Through yellow hallways.

Smile smile

With metal ball floating on lip.

Connected to tongue.

(when no one had one)

Long, long brown hair

Entangled with string.

Light lavender velvet—crushed material

Tucked beneath deep blue overalls.

Wallet connected to metal links

Hanging with gigantic safety pin.

Little china shoes

With delicate pink roses

Embroidered as though

Just for her.

Deep yearning eyes

Peering out into the world.

She could read an aura

And loved sugar cubes.

She rarely wouldn't smile.

Even when she had the blues

Elle Kovac

NAIVE IN THE 90'S

Living, loving and just trying to survive one of the craziest times in life...

Written (and lived) by Emilee Tran-MacGregor

To my family both near and far for more than I can list.

To those friends who took the time, energy and love

to read and be honest with me,

some of which found themselves reading about a past version of them.

And of course to my husband, the love of my life,

who has encouraged and supported this project throughout the process

and who knows this story from basically the start

but from a very different perspective.

I couldn't have made this happen without any of you.

I love you and am eternally grateful for you all.

May 2019

Dear Teenage Self,

Here we go little one. It has been almost 30 years since I have seen you, been you. And honestly, I don't even really remember that last time. You kind of just faded into "adulthood" with no acknowledgment or even a second thought.

In fact, if anything, I am pretty sure the passing of you was celebrated. Sad isn't it. You were a major part of who I was, and ultimately who I am. You were a huge impact on how I view myself, how I interact with others, how I accept and receive love, as well as how I give it and how I protect myself.

Yet somehow, even though you were so important, you have been lost, ignored, picked on and in many cases blamed for the insecurities and inner issues that have plagued my life since you were the one calling the shots. Now, in my 40's... excuse me while I have a moment saying that... IN MY FORTIES... *shudder *... Now, in my 40's I am starting to heal and have realized that our teen years are so very important and pivotal in shaping who we are as adults as well as how we interact with the world around us. From making friends, choosing lovers, career choices and opportunities. Everything.

So here we are, nearly 3 decades after the first words were written in "our" diary ready to meet again. I am ready to see you for real, through your own eyes, your own perspective for the first time in a very long time and now, through a different lens of life with a whole new view of the world and our self.

I will tell you, I am honestly a little scared and nervous. You and I weren't the best of friends, we've had a lot of issues along the way.
But I am now here, looking to understand you and maybe in turn, understand myself a little bit better.

Here we go little one. Nice to see you. Its been a long time. We have some catching up to do.

EMILY'S DIARY

STAY OUT!

ENTER AT YOUR OWN RISK

1992

May 4th, 1992 – Monday

I'm 15 today and still treated like a baby. I'm going out with Jake
for the 2nd time. We may actually love each other. Well I know I
love him. And I think it's the real thing. He's so sweet.
He's really shy, but that's OK I don't mind.

Today is my b-day! And it sucks! But I don't really care, in 7 days
on May 11th, will be 3 months for me and Jake! I love him so much!
But I have a problem. I still look at other guys! I must be like
massive scum.

For my b-day he gave me a gold bracelet It's beautiful.
I ♥ it, and him!

w/g/g ♥ Emily (8:45pm)

P.S. I think maybe Jake and I are getting too serious about each
other. I don't know. I mean I ♥ him but we are only 15.
What should I do? HELP! (10:12pm)

"...I'm worse at what I do best.
And for this gift I feel blessed,
our little group has always been
and always will until the end..."
~Nirvana

May 6ᵗʰ 1992 Wednesday

Today I went to the Dinner Theater to see 'Hooray for Hollywood' with the rest of the Drama Club for a field trip. It was pretty good. Jake went and so did Kim, Adam and Rob. As soon as Rob found out that Jake and I were still going out, he left the table. Then later when I said something about maybe breaking up with Jake, he kept going, "Break Up!" "Dump Him!"... ALL DAY! And I don't get it, cuz Rob is going out with someone. Adam was kinda acting weird too. I can't really explain it. I just don't understand boys. Oh well! (6:24pm)

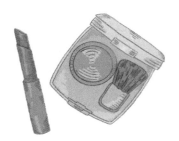

June 1st 1992 Monday

A LOT has happened since I last wrote. Like Mom and I are hardly talking. She's mad cuz I carved "JM" in my arm. She said that I did it even though she told me not to. But I did it a week before that talk!!! And why does she care about those? They aren't even deep, more like light etchings. It's not like she ever even cares enough or notices all my "cat scratches" and "mystery cuts" I do all the time. But this she has a fit over.
So now I really am a loner. All I have are my friends... and Jake. God only knows how long that's gonna last.

Besides that, a few weeks ago Tiffany and I got into a big fight. First she started lying to me to break me and Jake up. But I forgave her. Then she started talking about me behind my back! So last Thursday, May 28th, on Class Day, which is where we spend 5th period, lunch, 6th and 7th period outside like a Field Day. Me, and about 25 more people told her off for all sorts of stuff she's been doing. It was sooooooooooo funny. She had nothing in her defense. She was busted.

Oh yeah, another crappy thing that happened is Adam told me that he likes me and that I should dump Jake for him.

And when I told him that I only wanted to be friends, he got all mad at me and started to just yell at me right in the middle of art class! Just yelling at me telling me I was stupid and that he hated me AND... he called me a fucking gook...my dad being Vietnamese has NEVER been a problem for him before! He said it a bunch of times until Ms. P told him to calm down and sit in his seat. I just sat there and cried on my project. He said I was just a dumb gook and I should go just die in the jungle or fall on a grenade. No one even asked if I was ok. I just sat there and cried, ruining my drawing... my tears splattered all over it and smudged the pastels so bad I just threw it out. But oh well. Life sucks and then you die right? He was my friend. Or at least I thought he was. Sucks.

And THEN on the 27th Wednesday, we had Step Up Day at the high school. It's soooooooooooo big! I know I am gonna get lost.

On Saturday May 30th we (RFK Jr High) had our Semi! Kim, Zach, Aubrey, Jake and I got a limo. It was so cool!
The limo driver was pretty hot, so Aubrey asked him to the dance, cuz her boyfriend stood her up. Well the driver told her he couldn't cuz he was married!!! Hahaha!!
The dance was actually really fun. Jake and I didn't detach from each other hardly at all, ALL night. At one point, Bill came over to

us and goes, "It was soooo funny cuz you guys were slow dancing to Nirvana. It was great!"

I love Jake so much! When the Semi was over, the limo brought him home first, I was gonna go up with him to say good night and all (ya know!) We got to his steps and his mom opens the door (it was about 12:20 midnight) and says, "Hi! Jake did you get a picture?"

"Yes Mom."

"Jake honey, shoo the bugs away!"

Then she was just like standing there in the door... smiling.

So I said, "Well guess I gotta go! Bye!" cuz it definitely seemed like she wasn't going to leave, until I did. And I certainly wasn't going to kiss her son in front of her!

I couldn't believe it! It's like we have a no kissing relationship now. But oh well, I still ♥ him, it'll be 4 months on the 11th.

Sunday I was Confirmed and Mom gave me the cross necklace that Gram and Pops had gotten her. She also gave me a letter. I cried like a baby. She just left it on my bed. I didn't really see them at all. I actually spent the day over Kim's with her family at her Confirmation party. Must be nice to be celebrated. I wonder what that's like.

Anyways, I'll write more Friday cuz it's Class Night!

♥ – Emily ☺ SMILE!! I ♥ Jake a lot! (8:30pm)

June 5th/6th 1992 - 1am Fri/Sat

Tonight was Class Night. It was a blast! We got our yearbooks and they're pretty cool! Anyways, tonight or last night, was fun. I love Jake a lot!! And I think he loves me too!

Well, I gotta go to sleep. Write more soon!

☺ SMILE!

June 6th 1992- Saturday Night-

That "No kiss relationship" thing!! Never mind about that!!!

♥ – Emily

June 23 1992 – Tuesday

Well life sucks pud, big time here! Jake should have been home
Monday, well actually on Sunday night. But he's not coming back
until the 1st of July! I found out only because I had Ryan call
Jake's Mom to find out what time his plane was coming in, she said
he wasn't coming home until AT LEAST the 1st!!!
I am soooooooo mad! I mean he either lied to me, or didn't know he
was staying down there. And if he didn't know, why didn't he write
or call for even 5 seconds just to tell me he wasn't coming home.
I mean if Ryan hadn't found out for me I'd be sooooooo worried.
Now I'm mad. When he gets home and calls, he's going to wish he
stayed in Florida!!!

July 5th 1992 - Sunday

I don't know if I'm happy or sad. See yesterday "I" broke up with Jake. Even though I was the one to say it, he clearly was the first to think it and just had Ryan come by and get me to SAY the words so he doesn't have to feel bad.

The reason he stayed in Florida soooo long is cuz he said he met someone down there. She's "well developed" and has, I guess, the "perfect figure". And worst of all, is a model!!

I thought he loved me! I really did!! But oh well! I don't know if I should be upset or happy cuz I have been thinking about dumping him for a while now. But it still hurts so much! I thought I may have really loved him. I thought he loved me too. But I guess not since he came back on July 1st and he hasn't called and now all of this. I got all the info from Ryan. Like Jake had to make sure I knew all the stuff that would make me feel as bad about myself as possible, but he's way too much of a pansy to say it to me himself.

I'm sooooo mad. He could have called me and told me, but no. He left me hanging, sent his best friend to do his dirty work and made me say the official words. I don't know what to do. I keep telling everyone I'm fine, that I am glad this happened but inside I'm breaking up.

Kim isn't here, she's on vaca so there's no one I can tell how I really feel. I mean, I'm not sad we broke up, but he just extra hurt me by not telling me himself and making sure I knew all those details about her. Oh whatever. I'm really starting to hate Jake. I mean what a coward! He hurt me so bad. AND he told Ryan he did IT with her, WHILE we were still going out!! How could he have said he loved me one day before he left and then do this. I just don't understand. HELP!! ♥ – Me

Later on- July 5ᵗʰ 1992 – Sunday

I just re-read what little I wrote in this thing.
I guess I thought I was pretty "in love" with him, huh? Well that just shows how dumb I really am. I'm never letting myself love anyone again. Never. I'm not going to let anyone ever get close to me again. It's just not worth it.

August 14 1992 – Friday

So about a month ago Kim, her sister and her friend, Mr F. and 3 of his friends with 4 more kids, and I went to the beach. It ended up raining and being cold, so we didn't go swimming. Everyone was camping out in the two trucks and the station wagon having a pretty fun time just waiting to see if the rain was going to pass or at least let up. Singing songs, playing games. Just hanging out talking and laughing. But we were starting to get a little stir crazy.

So Kim and I decided to go to the boardwalk which was right across the parking lot. When we were almost there, this red car with two guys drove right up to us and they asked if we wanted a ride. We only had about 20 feet to go so we said, No.

Not to mention her Dad was watching the whole thing from the truck.

They go, "Where you going?"

And we said, "Up there." pointing to the boardwalk.

Then they just said, "Ok. Bye." and drove off!

We were like, Umm Ok?

Anyways they ended up meeting us down at the arcade and we found out they were: Brad – Cute! and Russell – Ugly

(actually Kim nicknamed him the Boogieman from Mars hahaha)!

We spent about two hours together. We had fun! But then we had to go because it was still raining and Mr. F. said if it still was at 1pm we were headed back home. Since I was staying over Kim's, she gave them her number. About an hour after we got back, Brad called. We ended up talking all day and all night. And even the next day too before I went home. He asked me to the movies. Unfortunately, I couldn't go. But he didn't give up. He asked again, and again, and again...and I couldn't.

It's not that I didn't want to. I did. But you know how strict my parents are. I think he thought I didn't like him and was just making up excuses. No one knows what life is like here...

So eventually, he stopped calling. Oh well, nothing I can do about it. My life is what it is. I have absolutely no control over it. Anyways, he lives in Westville, is 18 and works at Burger King. I don't think I will ever hear from him again.

September 13 1992 – Sunday

School started September 2nd. I'm now in the 10th grade and
officially in the high school. Finally!
I don't have a boyfriend, but I really don't want one. I mean I
don't want to be tied down to one person. I like a lot of people.
I still like Rob, who I kinda liked while I was going out with Jake,
ya know one of those reasons I always thought of maybe breaking
up with him.
And I like this guy Scott. He's a cool metal head Junior in my lunch,
geometry and study. There's also Dave, but he has a girlfriend...
so we won't get into that, especially because she and I are
starting to be really good friends I think. She's nice. I really like
her. So I don't want to mess that up. He's just super cute
though. Long light brown hair, blue eyes. But we're totally just
going to be friends.
There's also Joel. His nickname in German is Wolfgang,
so we all call him Wolfy. He's cute. I like him. The cool thing is, I
think he might like me a little too. I always catch him smiling at
me in class. He's got blue eyes, brown hair, and braces. But they
look totally cute on him.
The thing is Kim likes him, a LOT. So I don't know what to do.
Thank God she doesn't know I like him too.

I don't know what to do, so I won't do anything I guess. I also still like Kyle. I know, AGAIN! Yes, the same guy I was a little crazy over way back in 7th grade. So embarrassing. I was such a dork. Well, he's in three of my classes and he's still gorgeous. We talk all the time. Plus he and Chad were talking in German about girls they wanted to Do, and both of them pointed AT ME! I was shocked. And so embarrassed. I can't even look at them now.

There's probably more people I like too. The High School has SO MANY people in it, but I can't think of names right now.
So many boys. So much possibility. What do I do? ☺

September 14 1992 – Monday Morning

I have to go to school and I don't know what to do cuz I'm gonna
have to see all of those people I like AND Kim!
GOD HELP ME!

September 23 1992 – Wednesday

I still like Scott, Joel (Wolfy) and Rob. But now I'm "seeing" Brad!!
Yeah, it's the guy from the beach that stopped calling. Well he
called again! I saw him Saturday at the ski area! I went with
Kim, we snuck out and walked from her house. She got stuck with
the "Boogieman from Mars" (Russell) and some dude name Sam,
while Brad and I went off by ourselves. Not sure what they all
even ended up doing.

Brad and I had a good time. My lips were sore! So much kissing!!

w/g/g 🖤- me

October 3rd 1992 - Saturday

My life is over. Let me start at the beginning. There is this 12th grader, Trevor, since like the 2nd week of school that I thought was really cute. And now I heard he likes me too! But Aubrey likes him, A LOT, and has for some time. It's like all she talks about. So I don't know what's going to happen there if anything. As always, my feelings get put on the back burner.

Ok, to the bad stuff- I was taken to the police department today for threatening some girl with a knife at the Harvest Festival. Which, I really didn't do! See first these younger girls called Kim and I "Bitches", just for walking by. So we started walking after them cuz we wanted to know why. I mean seriously, who just calls random people bitches? Well, they started running and yelling all sorts of swears at us. So of course Kim yells, "Come on" at me, so we ran after them. We catch up to them and Kim pushed this one hoe a little, like shoved her to get her attention. They all start yelling at each other. And I'm just standing there. You know that just isn't the type of person I am. I'm just not a start shit type of girl. I can barely speak in class. I'd rather just blend into the background. But then Ryan comes running up. And before we know it, took out a knife, it was closed... but still definitely a knife.

Then just puts it IN my hand and says, "Hold this for me." and ran away! I didn't know what to do with it, so I just held it and stood there while Kim yelled at them, trying to figure out why they even said anything to us in the first place. I ended up just putting the knife in my pocket. I felt like such a dork just standing there holding it. They never answered Kim. And we just wanted to go back to our friends and have fun. So we just turned around and left.

Few minutes after we did, Ryan showed up again, got his knife back and then took off. Well, the little bitches called the police! And told them I threatened them with a huge knife. It wasn't! It was his boy scout pocket knife! Which I was just stupidly holding. It wasn't even open! I wasn't even the one getting all up in their faces or yelling! I was just standing there like a moron, along for the ride, getting called a bitch and look what happens!!

But apparently they believed them and I got taken down to the station in the back of a police car. Now my parents hate me.

I have no life. I can't use the phone. I'm grounded forever!

I can't even talk to my brothers, because I am "a bad influence".

They have been leaving sandwiches at the basement door for me.

And worst of all, I am not allowed to see Kim! She's my best friend and loves me more than even my own family. I hate it!

I'm getting out of here as soon as I'm 16!

I just gotta find a place to live! God HELP ME!

Sunday October 4th 1992

Monday I am asking some friends if I can move in with them. Wish me luck. I know if I leave I'll never be back and that makes me so sad. They may not love me, but I do love my family.

I feel like they have always hated me. Maybe if I left it would be best for all of us.

I don't know.

Mother, should I build the wall? -Pink Floyd

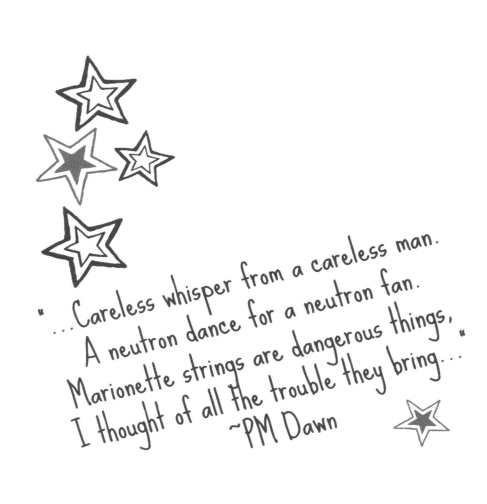

"...Careless whisper from a careless man.
A neutron dance for a neutron fan.
Marionette strings are dangerous things,
I thought of all the trouble they bring..."
~PM Dawn

November 16 1992 - Sunday

I'm still here. Life is pretty normal again, like the family shit and all. But I can't really go out much. Last night I did and it was NOT fun! I'll explain later! I g/g take a shower!! ♥ — Me

(Later, November 16 1992)

Ok I'll tell ya what happened when I went out. We went (Kim and I) to Aubrey's house and she LEFT us ALONE in the house. We were all suppose to go to a party. But she just left and didn't come back! When her brother Derrick came home, which was like 1:30am, he accused us of breaking into his room and kicked us out!! So we left, walked for about 1 hour until Scott and Kurt picked us up. We ended up going to Kurt's house. His Mom was really nice. Life Sucks.

xoxo

"Love deeply and passionately, you might get hurt,
but it's the only way to live completely."
~Leo Buscaglia

February 2 1993 – Tuesday

Well family life is normal and I'm not grounded but on "restricted activity" which means one or two times a month (maybe) I can go out. But I still can't talk on the phone. Which I really don't get why the phone is such a sore spot. Like why is me wanting to talk to my friends so offensive to my family? Well my friends don't act like they hate me, they actually WANT to talk to me, so of course I want to talk to them more. Key word here is MORE, not exclusively. Geez.

Not like Dad talks to me at all anyways. He straight up just ignores me. I say "Good Night" every night and I am lucky if he grunts in my direction. Usually it's just met with a furrowed brow and complete silence...

Anyways, a lot has happened lately. Rebecca is pregnant!
Like for real! A baby!! Wowzers!

Kim and Scott are going out. I hate the way she's changed for him and how he treats her soooo bad! He's called her every name meant for a slut, told her he doesn't trust her and a lot more. He's a friend of mine, but I hate him for what he's doing to her. I just hope she sees it before she gets hurt.

I'm not going out with anyone. Trevor, is still the guy
(12ᵗʰ grader from before) I like, but I have no idea what is going
on. Sometimes I think he likes me, like when he played the piano
just for me in the auditorium, and sometimes not. Aaaahhhhhh!
I'm sooooooooo confused. Plus Aubrey still REALLY likes him.
But oh well, I still (kinda) like Brad, oh course I haven't talked to
him in a while cuz I can't use the phone!! AND he's going to boot
camp soon! The Army. I may never see him again.

February 21, 1993 (past midnight-sun/mon)

Ok, much has happened. First, I HATE Scott! He is a fucking DICK! He treats Kim, like a piece of shit! And he's got this mondo fucking attitude. I'll start from the beginning.

From Feb 13 to today Feb 21, we have had Winter Break and I've stayed over Gram's. It was cool. Got to use the phone, watch tv, drink soda, eat frozen pizza, see my friends. On Friday I went out with Rob, Zach, Dean, Ian and Michael. It was really fun. Zach drove, he's fuckin' crazy! ☺ We got stuck up like a 4 foot snow bank and all this sorts of crazy shit! I spent pretty much all day with them. Around 8pm Michael got his car, so we went with him and he's fucking insane too!! We jumped a grass embankment, or snow bank in this case, at the high school parking lot. We fucking flew!!

Then on Saturday Ian, Dean, Rob and Zach wanted me to go hiking with them. They came to pick me up and I couldn't go, thanks to my Mom! But they stayed for an hour or so just to hang out. They asked if I thought maybe Kim wanted to go. So I called her and she got this attitude, kinda like, I'm above them! Actually she said, "Psssh, Hiking. Yeah right! Kim don't hike!" Which come on, we all know she does.

So Rob started to get mad, offended. I mean after all, he's been friends with us for years now. Then Scott got on the phone and started to yell at ME!

Screaming all this crazy shit, "If any of them touch her in any way, I'll find them all and fucking kill them!"

I was so confused and started to yell back at him saying, "Scott they're just friends. They don't want to DO anything with her. They just wanna go out for awhile, like we've done a million times. You should trust them they are our friends. What the fuck dude. Calm the hell down!"

"I'm just stating what I'll do if they touch her!"

"Well, that's bullshit! They're just friends!"

"Are you yelling at me??"

"No. I'm just stating something. You can't seem to hear anything else so I'm using a volume maybe you can." laughter from the guys. But the whole time they were just getting pissed, and I think hurt by Kim's lack of defending her friends to what looks like a crazy overprotective boyfriend.

So Kim got back on the phone and I asked her what the hell was that and she goes, "I don't know! I'm having the worst day." in this bitchy voice, like I'm suppose to feel bad for her and Scott. I cut it short and told her I had to go. The guys left, had fun, called me later and asked if I wanted to go to the movies.

Mom said no, of course, so Gram said they could come over. They did. Rob, Dean, Zach and Ian. We watched 'The Doors' in the living room. I sat on the couch and Ian sat with me. I ended up using his shoulder as a pillow.

Then he went to the bathroom and Dean sat down and held my hand. While they were waiting to rewind the tape, Ian and I kinda hugged, I put my head on his shoulder. He held on to me and put his head on mine.
Even Gram said we looked in love or something. I don't know about that, but he is really sweet. And he lives very close by so that's cool. But I kinda like Dean too. Aaahhhh. Confusion!
Well, Gram and I thought it best not to tell my mom. So she doesn't know. It's kinda weird keeping a secret from her, but hey what are ya gonna do?

Then today, Sunday, they all asked if I wanted to go sledding and of course, again, Mom said no. Why does she hate fun? Or does she just hate me having any?
So over the phone we got into a fight, we hung up. My guys showed up and I was crying. They tried to cheer me up. But whatever, I had to go home. Uncle Tom brought me in the truck.

He said if he got the job he wants, that he just applied for, then I could live with him and Gram! I think that's cool! But don't know about leaving my family. We might not get along, but I still love them. I don't know.

I'm confused, very confused about my family, my best friend, the guys, love, life, my emotions...

I think I'm having a nervous breakdown. GOD HELP ME!!!!

March 6th 1993

Well Rebecca is four months pregnant and you can really tell!
The doctor says she's too big and since it runs in her family,
they're gonna check for TWINS!!! Wow huh?! I think that's wild.
Um? Oh yeah one of my friends wants me to move in with her,
Amy. And I wanna go but I don't wanna lose my Mom or brothers,
even my Dad, though he's made it very clear he hates me just for
breathing... and of course the rest of my family. I know I'll leave
them eventually but I don't know.

Kim and I have kinda grown apart. We're still friends. And still say
Best Friends, but I don't know. It isn't even close to the same.
I think I really like Dean. We've been spending a lot of time
together. He really cares about me, what happens to me and what
I do to myself...the cutting, the eating and stuff. He's so sweet.
g/g c-ya ♥ -me

March 27 1993 - Saturday ☺

Rebecca's huge! When she sits, she bulges. It's sooooooo cute!!
Oh and just the little thing of, I'm in love!! (OK maybe not love
but strong like like?) No! Not with Dean. He's the biggest dick.
I stopped liking him because he said he cared and all. But than he
got pissed over the stupidest things and all jealous. I don't need
that. I get enough attitude at home. So I told him to fuck off
and stay outta my life.

Anyways, I went over Amy's house last weekend with Krissy.
It was great. And it changed my life. I'm soooo much closer to
them now! I mean, I can tell them anything and they said the
same! I'm really happy.
As before, Kim and I are still friends but not as close and drifting
apart. It's sad. It happens and I know that. We've been best
friends for 6 years!! But we have both changed so much. I just
hope I never lose her completely. I think I would die if I did.

So anyways, I love James. (Ok, maybe not "love" But I REALLY
like him.) He's a junior and he's great! Over the weekend I really
got to know him and on Wednesday March 24th, we started going
out. He's so nice! But I think we may have kinda rushed into
things.

I mean I really don't know him that well and vise versa. I really like him so far though. I'm just afraid he's gonna get to know the real me and not like it. I don't like me. And then what happens if we break up and we hate each other? We're gonna have a little problem. See his best friend is Dave, who Amy is involved with and what if... aaaahhhh!!

Well I hope we don't break up, but who knows right?
Maybe I worry too much. ♥ -Me

P.S. I gotta go on a diet! I'm REALLY fat! Maybe I'll get diet pills!!

"My face is my fortune, that's why I'm totally broke."
~Bette Midler

Saturday April 3rd 1993

Hey Chickens, it's Saturday. Last night was the "Sadie Hawkins Dance" and James asked me to it. I know, the girl is suppose to ask the guy but I don't know, I just am not that girl.

Anyways Thursday I asked and Mom said she'd have to check with my Father. Well Thursday night James got his car wrecked (no one was hurt and it was the other person's fault). No car meant he couldn't bring me and Amy, so after school we went to my house to get my stuff. Her mom drove us.

I went in and only my father was there. I told him I was going home with Amy to get ready for the dance. He said Ok. And literally only that. If he didn't want me to go I am sure he would have said it. He's had no problem doing so in the past... but whatever.
So I honestly thought it was, especially since Mom had said she was fine with it as long as he was.
I mean he SAID the word, "O-K." What more did she expect me to get from him? A signed permission slip?? Well I left a note for my Mother letting her know where I was and what was going on.

Then at 3:30, I called, just to make sure she got the note and she was PISSED. She hung up on me!! But I went to the dance anyways and I had a good time! So because of the note and phone thing, I couldn't go over Amy's this week for spring vacation, like we had planned. I think I have been re-grounded. It's only the first day of vacation and I already miss James and my friends.

April 19 1993 — Monday

James is so sweet. I know I say stuff like that about all the people I like then I take it back. But he's different. I want to spend all my time with him! I may even want to have sex with him!! I love him I think. The 24th is one month and hopefully the first of many many more ☺ I completely trust him. well g/g!

Later on: April 19 1993

I was thinking about James, and every time I can't help but smile. whenever he holds me I feel sooooo safe, so loved. I hope we last a long, long, long time. The only thing that scares me, is he does soooo many drugs. I'm just afraid he's gonna get hurt. Or worse! If he does I think I would die.

Another thing that makes me sooooo happy is Amy said that he had to get really drunk or high to touch any of his ex girlfriends. we are always hugging or kissing or something... it makes me happy to think we must be different to him, I must be different to him.

Amy also said he never smiled and always looked upset when his girlfriends were around. With me he's always (well most of the time) smiling. So I guess he's happy too. AND Amy said he talks about me all the time. So I'm happy, actually I'm very happy.

He makes me feel so great and he's got the greenest eyes, they are so nice. And his hair is beautiful! You know what a sucker I am for long hair. God, I like him sooooo much! I just hope I don't fall too hard and then to be quite blunt, get fucked over. I don't think I could handle getting hurt again.

Maybe I shouldn't let myself get too attached.

well g/g ♥ – Me

April 22 1993 – Thursday

Ok, first of all I'm really confused. Today... no, let's start from the beginning. All Spring Break I kissed major parental ass and it worked! I got my phone back! ☺ Dad's idea!!! Shocker, I know!! Well today I received my first call in 7 months from Brad!!! Yes! Brad from the beach and the ski area.

At first I was like really surprised but happy. We were talking about just this and that and he goes, "I missed you, a lot." in this really soft voice and I was kinda shocked. But I told him I missed him too! Cuz it was, is true. No matter what, he was important to me. (I can't believe I wrote that even as I look at it. I don't know where it came from, it just slipped out... kind of like when he and I were talking too. What is wrong with me?)

And then he goes, "You sound happy to be talking with me."
I was like, "Yeah I am I suppose."
And he said, "Why?"
"Cause I thought you forgot about me."
"I couldn't forget about you, you know that don't you? Never."
And all this really sweet shit. I was like wow!

Well I said this was all confusing me and he goes,

"You weren't confused that night at the ski area, were you?"

I go, "No. That was one night I wasn't."

Then we just started to talked about dumb stuff because I didn't

know what to say or do.

We eventually got on the subject of how we met and he goes,

"I remember when we first met at the beach"

"Me too. It was raining."

And he says, "Yeah, it was a day just like today."

It was actually exactly like today. Gray, kinda warm, a little cool

breeze and dreary with rain. I changed the subject so fast

because the vibe was getting super heavy.

Then he was talking about his weight lifting and said how he was

bigger muscles wise and gained 50 more pounds than when I last

saw him and it was muscle, six pack and all.

I'm like, "I lost 4pds." just kinda being dumb.

He goes,"why?"

I say, "Because I'm fat"

He's like, "No. You're perfect!"

"No, I am and was fat!"

"To me you are and were perfect."

"You're so silly." I was getting very uncomfortable.

"No. Really. You are everything."

we dropped it because I just didn't know what to say to that. And he could tell I was getting uncomfortable. So we talked about nothing important for awhile. Then I had to go.

He confuses me. He made it seem like he still likes me. But Kim says he's got a girlfriend. And I guess a very serious one. I don't know. And I feel guilty cuz I think I was kind of unfaithful to James, I mean I went along with all of it. Said somethings I probably shouldn't have...

I feel so bad. I'm tired, upset and wanna go to bed.
I'll write more tomorrow if anything happens. w/g/g ♥ – Me

P.S I forgot, he played the song, "If I ever fall in love again" by Shai for me.

"The Truth is rarely pure and never simple." ~Oscar Wilde

May 21 1993 – Friday

Well I'm still with James and I think I may really love him.
I mean I want to sleep with him. Not because I am afraid to lose
him if I don't, he's never pressured me for anything, it's because
I think I really want to.
Actually I think about it a lot. We were going to have sex May 7th
but I couldn't sleep over. We went to Billiards instead. Then I
tried for today but, no. Again. So I'm trying for tomorrow. I think
my Mom knows though and that's why I can't get out.

Can I tell you a little secret though? A small part of me almost
doesn't mind. I'm a little nervous about it, being my first time and
all. But oh well, I really do love him, I think. I mean I've never
felt this way before, about anyone. And it's what you are suppose
to do, right? I don't know.

Plus, I am also so scared for him all the time. He does soooo many
drugs. I don't want him to die on me, or even get hurt. I don't
know. It's complicated. His ex-girlfriend, Vanessa, also formally
Amy's Best Friend, actually made a point to come up to me in the
hall one day.

She told me that all he cared about was drugs, and to be careful.
Then Michael said this other time, that James loved drugs too
much to love anyone else for real.
I don't know. It's really kinda scary.

But it's not like he's some stumbling drooling fool. He's funny.
And smart. Kind and sensitive. At least most of the time.
And even when I've seen him cross eyed, he's harmless and just
kinda funny-weird. I don't know. I'm just confused on all levels
possible, about all things possible. Well, g/g do homework.
♥ ya- Emily

I ♥ James   Amy ♥'s Dave

May 23 1993 – Sunday

Yesterday I went to Amy's with James and Dave. Well, Dave left after a little bit and James stayed for a while longer and just hung out.

Later Amy and I went to Billiards to meet up with Lily and Anne. At like 10pm Amy and I went to Game Room One, for a Tyrant Trooper concert. Amy's ex boyfriend, Alec, who use to abuse her, was suppose to fight with Dave.
When we got there, we found out that Alec had passed out somewhere. I found James and was happy. Amy told a whole bunch of people what Alec had done to her.

A little bit goes by and he showed back up, crawled out of whatever hole he had been in and some guy Martin punched him! Then Kyle started with him, smacked him right upside the head, it was great!
Alec got pissed and started to yell at Dave for it, like Dave got everyone to pick on him or something. Alec looked like he was going to cry! Anyways right before we left, Amy went up to him and slapped him REALLY hard, right across the face. It was great!

I guess he's also got like all these Latin Kings after him and his friends. It's so cool! Don't hit girls jerk!

Then Amy's mom brought me home. She had the truck, and we all couldn't fit, so the boys (Dave and James) sat in the front and Amy and I laid in the back. It was cold, but fun. We talked, laughed and watched the stars pass by. It was like magic.

well, g/g! ♥ – Me

"...You're safe from pain in the dream domain, a soul set free to fly. A round trip journey in your head..." ~Queensryche

5/26/1993

¼ of a Brain Cell

I only have ¼ of a brain cell left inside of my head.

It's filled with thoughts of pink flowers

Growing on purple moss in the winter.

Do chickens dance naked in the moonlight?

How come there aren't any purple marshmallows?

What really happens when you die?

Where do you go?

Why are we here?

If all of this is happening in a ¼ of a brain cell,

Could you imagine what would happen if I had an entire brain?

I can!

"Sweet blossom come on under the willow,
we can have high times if you'll abide.

We can discover the wonders of nature,
rolling in the rushes down by the riverside."

-Grateful Dead

June 20th 1993 – Sunday – Father's Day

Hi! I haven't written in a LONG time. But a lot has happened.
Amy slept with this guy Al to get back at Dave for sleeping with
Bethany the Bitch. Now Dave says he hates Amy. But I don't
believe him, I think he's just hurt, even though HE slept with
Bethany first. I don't know. Boys!
Well she went out with this guy Chris for a minute, and NOW she's
with Jared. All this happened in like 3 weeks!!

I'm still with James. But I'm not sure how much longer. I mean
I really don't think he's into me or this relationship at all.
He would rather go out with Dave and Bethany wherever, than
his own girlfriend. And I can't go out that much, so when I can
you'd think he'd make a point to see me. I can almost feel over the
summer we're not going to keep in touch.

So there goes another one. God it hurts. I love him.
I don't know what I'm gonna do. It hurts just thinking of losing
him. But it may actually hurt more being with him.
I'm so confused.

Thank God I have my girls Amy, Lily, Krissy, Anne, Esther...
All of them! And Rebecca, she is a COW!! Only a little more than
2 months!! Sept 2nd she is due. It's soooooooo wild!

Hmmm, what else. Kim and I hardly talk anymore. I kinda miss
her. But whatever.
Also, I've got finals this week. Wednesday Lily, Esther, Amy and I
are suppose to go to the beach since it's a half day and we will be
done! I can't wait! Maybe I will forget about James for a while.

I have to go. Chow!! ♥ — Emily

June 26 1993 – Saturday

Hi! It's SUMMER!!! No School!! But I'm kinda upset, cuz that also means I can't see my friends much at all. I can't even say how sad that makes me. They are my everything. My sanity.

I'm still with James. 3 months, 2 days. We haven't had sex yet. But if I work my parents right, there will be more than regular fireworks for the 4th of July!! I can't wait!! I'm scared but excited at the same time.

I'm scared it's gonna hurt and I'm gonna make a fool of myself or something. I know people assume I have experience because it seems like everyone else does, but I don't. So I can't even really talk to my friends about it because it just makes me feel like a baby.

But oh well, I love him. I've never felt this way about anyone.

And I'm pretty sure no one has ever felt like he does about me, or at least how it seems he feels... most of the time.

Anyways on July 1st it's Rebecca's baby shower and I don't have any money to get her anything. I feel soooo bad!

Well, It's past 12 so I guess it's Sunday the 27th.

I'm tired so I'll write more some time soon. Love, Emily

July 1st 1993 – Thursday

Rebecca had her baby shower today. It was pretty fun! I was happy for her. Only 2 more months before she pops! Can't wait to meet the baby! I'm still with James, but um, I don't know, cuz today Aubrey said she saw him at a party with Dave and Bethany, And that James was "with" some other girl.

I don't know what to think or do... I think I'm gonna die.

Amy said it could have been just one of Bethany's friends there with her. I don't know, even the idea hurts. But as Tiffany said, If it hurts too much to be with him, there's not much I CAN do but end it. I just don't think I can handle breaking up with him!! AAAHHHHHHHHHH!!!! well g/g ♥ – Me

P.S I got Rebecca a little nightgown (baby in a bag) and a snowsuit for 6-12 months. She loved them... The crazy part? Mom was who brought me out to get them AND she paid for them. It was so cool of her. I don't know why it happened. But I'll take it.

July 7th 1993 - Wednesday

Well today I went to the beach with Kim!! God it was fun! But I fell asleep and now I'm so burnt! It hurts A LOT! Anyways it was like the old days. It made me happy. I've missed her so much.

It's weird how someone can be so important to you. Be such a huge and impactful part of your life and then you hardly see them.

Anywho Kim and Scott finally broke up. Thank goodness! She and Brandon are kinda going out, so she's happy. He makes her happy. And that makes me happy. It's cool having her as a friend again. I missed her.

Amy is in the Berkshires for a while (until the 11th). I'm going crazy without her.
For some reason I think Esther is mad at me. But I can't think of why she would be. I guess I'll call her tomorrow.

Ummm... oh yeah. I haven't said anything to James about what Aubrey said. He hasn't called in five days. Maybe he's mad too or maybe he found someone else and just doesn't care enough to tell me it's over.

why does this keep happening to me. What is wrong with me.
I don't understand why no one can just love me for me.
Am I just absolutely unlovable? well, g/g. ♥- Emily

P.S we're going to Cali July 20- August 18 to visit with the Viet
family! I don't wanna leave for that long!!

" ...Said I think I'm losing my mind, this time.
This time, I'm losing my mind..." ~ Beastie Boys

July 8th 1993 — Thursday

Well, Esther's not mad. She called today! So I'm happy.

She and Calvin are having problems, again. Which sucks. I hope they work things out. I hate seeing her sad. And she's sad a lot lately.

What else, oh yeah. Kim told me Randy has been calling Lily a whore and Esther said the same a long while ago, like right after they started going out. But I don't understand!! They've been together for a little more than six months and they always seem happy.

I really don't understand. People are so confusing. Why do they all just keep hurting each other? I want to go kick Randy if it's true. Why would he talk about her like that?

She is awesome. And beautiful. She loves him. Sometimes I don't think he deserves her. But I won't ever tell her that. Because I couldn't take it if she got mad at me.

He better not hurt her for real, cuz then there will be problems...

On a better note, I may go see 'Riders on the Storm' on the 12th with Amy and hopefully we will get to meet up with everyone.
I hope so!!

I called James, but he wasn't home, like always. Oh well, life sucks.

I'll try tomorrow. w/g/g ♥- Emily

August 25 1993 — Wednesday

Well, we are home from CAL! And I didn't write in here at all!
Hold on, 'Runaway Train' by Soul Asylum is on and I love it!

"Got a ticket for a runaway train. Like a madman laughing at the rain. A little outta touch, little insane. It's just easier than dealing with the pain..."

That's such a great song, I feel it deep in my veins. I want to runaway all the time. From everything.

Anyways, Cali was OK I mean, it was a family vacation so it did get boring sometimes. I met some cool people, watched Dracula like a million times on free pay preview, ate some good food and hung out with my cousins and all CA family. It was pretty cool.
But I did miss James and my friends so much. James had gone camping at the beach two weeks before I left. Then I was gone for a month, so it was like aaaahhhh!!!! But when he did get back from his vacation, he wrote me a letter and it was soooooooooo sweet!!! He said stuff like "I miss you... been too long since I've seen ya... Can't wait for ya to get back... I Love You" I was so happy that I started to laugh and cry at the same time.
I love him soooo much!!

Anyways I found out he had to chop his mop. Only to his shoulders, but still it was a shock! He got two D's on his report card so his Dad made him cut it. Rrrrrrr!!

Amy and Dave are friends again, Thank god! Cause it was weird and awkward with them not talking and being all angry. Esther and Calvin broke up, but are going out for the 4th time!! She's happy they worked it out.

Yesterday Esther, James, Dave, and Amy came over. We copped a squat in a circle in my driveway for a few hours. I was SO happy just to be with them, that they came to see me, that maybe they missed me too.
Dave is the same old silly Dave. I still love him, like my brother... ok my hot step brother maybe, just don't tell anyone I said that. He is going out with Bethany again (gag).

Amy was going out with Chris but ended up falling for Dan. But then he dumped her after 1½ days! I don't know what happened really, but he's going to MA for college so it's better that way. And I think she is better off, clearly he didn't appreciate her the way he should.
She, Amy, cut her mop too! To her shoulders.
It looks so good!! But it was a shock!

Hmmmm, let's see. What else... I almost broke up with James before vacation (CA) and almost went with Jared but decided not to because I love James too much. It's not James's fault that I can't go out and that he has a life.

Oh yeah, Kim is now officially going out with Brandon. She's also super happy her parents are getting a divorce. Her mom is such a monster. Maybe now she can get away from her and her abuse. Rebecca is still a cow. But so cute. No Baby YET!!

School starts Sept 1st.

'Riders on the Storm' at the park August 30th. Can't wait!
It's going to be a blast!

Well, that's about it. Oh except that yesterday was 5 months for me and James! ♥- Me

P.S OH YEAH!! I forgot!! Lily's pregnant!! About 3 months.
She's keeping the baby. Randy is HAPPY. Wants to name it Floyd!!
Girl or Boy! The dude is so BURNT!

"Hello me, meet the real me and my misfits way of life. A dark, black past is my most valued possession

Hindsight is always 20-20 but looking back, it's still a bit fuzzy." -Megadeth

August 28th 1993 – Saturday

Well I haven't talked to James or Esther since Tuesday when they came over. I'm kinda afraid that they're mad or something.
And maybe Lily is mad too? I've tried to call but no one ever answers and she never calls. I hope they aren't. I know a lot of stuff is going on. And I can't think of any reason for them to be, but who knows. Sometimes it feels like I am disposable.
Or like no one really likes me, but just tolerates me. I don't know.
Maybe I am just crazy.

Anyways three days until school. Ummm... hmmm... What else.
Oh, I don't know if I'm gonna be able to go to 'Riders on the Storm' Monday. First cuz I don't know if Dad will let me, or should I say I don't think Mom can convince him. Plus I don't know how I'm gonna get there!! I don't have any idea. But oh well.
Hoping it works out!!
I'll write more when I find out what's going on. Later.

"Oh, let the sun beat down upon my face and stars fill my dream.

I'm a traveler of both time and space to be where I have been.

To sit with elders of the gentle race, this world has seldom seen.

They talk of days for which they sit and wait, all will be revealed."

-Led Zeppelin

August 30 1993 – Monday

Well, I went to the 'Riders on the Storm' concert. It was wild!
I went with Amy, and we got there like 6:30pm. We found the
Freaks (Esther, Lily, Anne, Randy, Chunk-whose real name is
Charles...I'm actually not sure why they call him Chunk, he's not at
all chunky in ANY way...and Robin, Calvin, Krissy....etc) and we were
the first on the little stage thing to be dancing.
It was wild and amazing. The weather was gorgeous. The music
was magic. My best friends and I dancing like crazies. Perfection.
I didn't find James (and the rest of the guys; Dave, Jim, Chad,
Kyle, Cory...etc) until the intermission. But that's OK when I DID
find them, I was happy. God I love him! I'm sooooooo happy.
Today was all the fun♥

School starts Wednesday I'm nervous and I don't even know why.
Anyways, family is actually going pretty good too, for once. Dad and
I are actually talking. I don't know what happened or why.
But I'll take it while I can get it. It's nice. I miss my Dad.
We use to be so close. Oh well.

I think I'm mildly drunk. My head is pounding.
But I can't stop smiling. g/g! ♥ – Me

September 9 1993 – Thursday

Rebecca had her baby!!! It's a girl.
Her name is Ashley Katelyn Conners!
I'm so happy for Rebecca!!!

September 19 1993 – Sunday

I went and saw Ashley Wednesday (the 15th). Oh she is sooooooooo cute and soooooooo small!! I'm so happy for Rebecca!

Anyways, I had a fight with Mom a while ago and it actually ended up working out. I think she may have actually heard me for once. Now I have an 11pm curfew and can go out pretty much every week. So that's super cool.

Friday I went out with Chad, Amy, Robin, Kyle, Aubrey and James. We went to Laser Zeppelin at the planetarium.
It was wild. we had A LOT of fun! I really love James!

On Friday in homeroom we voted for the theme song for the JR Prom. I voted for Angel by Aerosmith. It won!!!
The prom is December 4th. I can't wait! I wrote a note to James asking if he'd go with me. I hope he does! Well I g/g! ♥ - Emily

November 12 1993 – Friday

Well I got a lot to tell you!! First, Lily is now, um, lets see...
five months pregnant and she got kicked out of her house and is
now living in an apartment with Randy downtown. It's small but
cute. She seems happy. But I don't know, I worry about her.
All the time.

Onto Esther, she is no longer at home either. She also got kicked
out! She lives with Calvin now, who of course lives in Westville, so
she doesn't go to school anymore. I miss her, A LOT.
I hope she comes back.

Amy and I had a fight. But we're friends again, kind of, but things
are definitely not the same. It sucks. Why do people fight over
stupid things? And why do we always hurt and get hurt by those
we love the most. I miss what we were.

Ok, James. I love him and "said" it. SO DID HE! I'm so happy
about that! He said he wouldn't say it unless he meant it.
So that's super cool. Ummm, tonight, we finally tried to have sex.
It hurt. And didn't exactly work out. He was wonderful about it.

I am so embarrassed and was then too. But he was just so sweet and kind.

One thing is lodged in my brain, that I wish I could stop thinking about. I saw a letter that he got from some girl June, from MA. And right next to it I noticed a letter he wrote to her. They were just laying out for the whole world to see, but I didn't read them. I did see the end of it though and it was signed, "Love James".

Now maybe that doesn't count for anything, but still, he can write a fucking letter to someone but never notes to me? And "Love"? I don't know. I guess I'm being a jealous bitch. But seeing that upset me!

I don't know, maybe I'm overreacting!! I just don't know. It's hard to explain. I do love him and I'm just so scared that I'm gonna lose him like I seem to lose anything and anyone I love. AAAHhhhHHHH!! w/g/g ♥ ya- Emily

12/3/1993

Love is...

Love doesn't mean a thing if the person you love,

Doesn't feel the same.

Love is for fools meant only to give heartache and shame.

Love is like an everlasting scar.

Love is the tears you cried, when he's gone away far.

Love is the painful truth that you found out he lied.

Love is the nights that all you could do was cry.

Love is pain, but not always sorrow.

For after those long lonely nights,

There is always a tomorrow.

December 24th 1993 – Friday – Christmas Eve

Well I got LOTS and LOTS to tell you!

Today is James and my 9 month anniversary! I'm really happy!

Last night I spent the day over his house cuz we had a ½ day of school. We were in the fort and we were talking, all the others (Dave, Dustin, Jim...) were joking around with each other.

James and I were just talking together. He was paying attention to me like I was the only one there. Or at least like the only one who mattered. I said I was cold and he goes, "If you're cold we can go back to my house for awhile, ya know I'd do anything for you." I was like Awww! ☺ He makes me so happy. He wrote me a letter and he told me how much he really does love me. He makes me feel sooooooo special. No one has ever made me the priority. It's so weird.

On December 4th we went to the prom. He looked soooo good in his tux! I was like, Wow! We had a lot of fun. We went with Kris, Chad and Dave. Tiffany, Amy and a few others were at our table too. Krissy wore my semi dress. She looked so pretty. Part way through she changed her shoes, into her red converses!! It was great! I'll never forget the smile on her face while she did the Electric Slide in those ratty old things and my black lace poofy dress.

Total coolness.

The girl is a classic waiting to happen and she doesn't even see it...
But eventually she had her boyfriend, Clint, pick her up.

Oh yeah, Dave and I danced a slow dance, he said he had been waiting all night to. Honestly, I thought that was a little weird... but nice. It made me smile.

After prom we dropped him off at the "cool kids" party. I mean he IS practically one of "them". The rest of us went to a different one at Luke's. It was a really fun night.

Yesterday James gave me my Christmas present. I got a big white teddy bear dressed like Santa and a silver necklace with a heart charm! I love them!

Let's see? Oh yeah, Esther is back!! And she is also pregnant!!!
I know, what is going on??? She's living at Calvin's grandmother's now, which is in town. So she's in school again. Thank goodness.
She misses her family though. Hopefully they will come around.
Lily is still prego too. 6 months.
Kim and I are good friends again, so are me and Amy. Thank goodness.
But I think I'm closest to Kris now. We've been spending a lot of time together. Lots of notes. Lots of talking... about everything. She's so amazing. She never judges, just supports and stands up for those she loves. But now she's leaving.

She's moving to Newford for a little bit to be closer to the club, then traveling the country on tour. I'm kind of upset about it but trying to keep positive and supportive. After all she's helped me with a lot of problems. She's so easy to talk to. I'm really gonna miss her a lot. But she will be back this summer, so it's all good.

Well, I think that's about it. Ummm, family life still sucks.
Oh yeah! I found out who June is. She's a girl that James and Noah (his cousin) met in New Hampshire when they went camping. He told me all about it all by himself. I didn't even tell anyone about the letters I saw... Of course that doesn't explain the "Love" part. But he loves me. And I trust him. I think. I mean. I want to. I'm just overthinking. Like always. Anyways g/g. C-ya!
            Love, Emily

P.S. It looks like we are finally gonna have a white Christmas!
Its been long enough!

January 1st 1994 – Saturday

HAPPY NEW YEAR!!! Well, this year has already started shitty.
First on Thursday, December 30th 1993, the Fort got busted!
James, Cory, Nick, and Dustin (Dave wasn't there thank god!
He just happened to be on an "errand").

They got caught with a bong and two bowls. They weren't arrested there but the police are getting arrest warrants. They also called their parents.

James now has a 9pm curfew and he had to cut his hair, like for real!!! He is turning himself into the police on Monday. All the guys have to go to court.

I am just happy that none of them had weed or trips on them! James said he will probably only get fined or community service. But oh well, I guess it was kind of bound to happen. At least he has to stay straight for a while.

I still love him, though honestly it's very hard sometimes and I am really starting to have major doubts.

g/g cuz I'm tired. ♥ Emily

" This is the strangest life
I've ever known "
~The Doors

1/11/1994

Struggling

All I do is smile all through the day.

Hiding my feelings,

Throwing my sanity away.

It seems to everyone that my spirit is high.

But behind my mask of happiness,

I'm struggling to get by.

Death is all I think of,

To get rid of this hidden pain.

Tears of sorrow run down my cheeks,

Like the warm spring rain.

Finally unable to take the pain anymore,

I walk with Death through his darkened one way door.

January 22 1994 – Saturday

Once again a lot has happened. James hasn't been arrested yet.
But Cory's mom called the police yesterday to see what was going
on and the police said a few more weeks. James had his hair cut.
Wow. At first it was a TOTAL shock. But now that I've gotten
use to it, I guess I kinda like it.

Anywho, Rebecca is coming back to school Thursday with Ashley in
the Baby Room. I can't wait! There is are like 20 people pregnant
in school. That's insane!! What the hell is happening??
Hmmm. Kim and I are really good friends again and that makes me
happy. Oh yeah, Chad is determined that I am going to marry
him. I don't think so!!! Dude is crazy.

I almost broke up with James. First what happened is, for some
reason I can't eat in front of him. It embarrasses me. So he made
it up in his head that I'm anorexic. NOT EVEN CLOSE!
Look at how fat I am! Gosh, even my eyelids are fat!! Well, last
Friday January 14th, he said that he didn't know if he wanted to
"stay with an anorexic person".
It really hurt and made me mad. Who says something like that?
What if I was? He'd just get rid of me??

That isn't love, no matter how many times he says he loves me. Well, he didn't call Sat or Sun. Then we had Mon off and he didn't call either. Tues we had a snow day and he FINALLY called.

All weekend I thought that he had decided to really get rid of me. He said he "tried" to call. I don't know about that, but I do KNOW that everyone else got through. I was so pissed! I wrote him a note saying he'd better tell me right now what the hell was going on and where I stood in his life! And how what he said really hurt me. He wrote a very sweet note back and I was happy (this was on weds during school).

Then after school Chad was bringing me home from my detention and he messed up and told me that he was headed over to James's and they were gonna try PCP or ANGEL DUST, with those jerk Abbot brothers!! I was sooooo pissed!!! That stuff can KILL YOU.
It's not like weed or even trips, it's dangerous, FOR REAL!

Well the next day James didn't say anything about it. So at lunch I got mad and started to yell at him. Then cry. He thought the whole thing was pretty damn funny! Which just pissed me off even more.

Then he had the nerve to say, "You weren't suppose to know about it, but since you do..." and just started laughing.

That hurt so bad. I mean if he was gonna hide THAT from me, what else hasn't he told me or what else WILL he hide? And so unapologetic and just cruel.

I ended up going over his house after school yesterday and we had a talk. He said he didn't like it, it was too addictive, bad and dangerous. That if he had known just how bad it was before, he wouldn't have done it. Then he told me how much he cared for me and all this other shit.

So I was happy, I guess. I mean what can I do? He's his own person. I can't make him do or not do anything. But it also leaves a lot of questions and doubt in my mind about him.

And ultimately, about us.

Anyways, we went out with Evan and Paul at like 7pm and went to these dudes apartment over the Blue Parrot. They were crazy but I guess you kind of have to be to live above a strip club nicknamed the Dirty Bird!!! ☺ We stayed for about an hour, then we went to Luke's for a keg party. That was really fun!

Lets see who was there... Anne, Lily, Jim, Cory, Robin, Esther, Aubrey, Chunk, and a bunch of other people, plus a few I didn't know. It was REALLY wicked!

About 9:30pm James and I were laying on the couch, he had his head on my chest, I love when he lays like that. But anyways, he kissed me then goes, "I love you. I've wanted to say that all night. But I was too shy to." It made me smile.

We were talking about Chad, and how he's always writing me poems, and notes, saying things. And I guess it's really bothering James. He heard how Chad had said he wanted to marry me.
I told him that he was harmless and James goes,
"Well, maybe I'll marry you! Yeah! That would be good."
Later we were talking about how school is halfway over (we have midterms Mon, Weds, Thurs), how he's gonna go to college and how I was worried cuz he would probably find someone new. He goes, "I'll tell you right now. I deliberately check out other chicks and I ALWAYS think how lucky I am to have you. Everyone else is not for me."

I do still love him and now I know he really loves me too. He even said he doesn't mind that I don't do drugs and am pretty straight edge. Actually everyone is pretty damn cool about it.
Like the people at the Blue Parrot, they clam baked in a room and I got buzzed just from being in there, but they all were very cool about me not actually smoking.

At like quarter to 6am James and I left, we just wanted to go get some sleep. We started walking to his house since it's not far from school, he didn't drive, and his parents dropped us off.
We walked for about 5mins and then his mom picked us up.

Just between us, I don't like her. I'm never Emily, I'm always "Her" or "She". Blah blah blah. Whatever.

Anyways we got to his room and I fell asleep at like 6:30am, woke up at like quarter after 9 and James woke up like, maybe 30mins later. I felt so sick. I didn't throw up or anything, my stomach just killed. Yuck first hangover! I went home about 10:30am.

Later, I was on the phone with James and he said something about only 2 hours of sleep and I go, "It was more wasn't it? Cause I fell asleep like around 6/6:30."
He goes, "I know. I didn't fall asleep until like 7."
I was like, "What did you do for the half hour?"
And he goes, "I was just watching you sleep."
I was like Ooooooooo ☺ But also I felt stupid.
I feel so ugly around him.

Well, anyways, Robin called today. She's not in school anymore. Which sucks! Her parents pulled her.

February 6th 1994 – Sunday

Friday was the overnight thing. It was pretty cool. It started out pretty bad though, just sooooooo boring. Let's start from the beginning.

I went over James's house at like 6pm. His Dad picked me up after bringing James to the police station to turn himself in cuz they finally just processed the warrants. So moods weren't exactly light. Now he's got court the 21st.

We got to his house, and Dave called. So we went there for a few minutes since it's right across the street. Then Dave just came back over James's with us and we had rum and cokes YUM!
This was about 7:30pm. And DAMN did I get wasted. I couldn't see straight. My head was pretty much floating and let's not talk about walking! Which of course we had to do right after my last glass. We had to go to where the old fort was, yup they had to take it down after it was busted, to meet up with Dustin.
I couldn't even handle standing. Well we went home, then to the dance. The first one and a half hours sucked pud! REAL bad! It was just really boring, nothing going on. Eventually it picked up and got better.

which I was glad about. Some people get weird about it and start yelling Narc.

Anyways, not this Friday but NEXT Friday, February 4th, is an overnight dance. I think I'm going! I know James is. It's for the Muscular Dystrophy Association. It sounds pretty cool! There's gonna be a DJ and 92 WPBF is gonna be broadcasting from the gym. There's gonna be games. And in the atrium is gonna be movies and free food! ALL NIGHT! And then breakfast!
It should be fun! w/g/g! ♥ me

P.S. Monday will be 10 months for me and James ☺

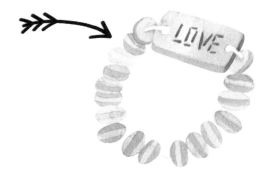

And she might be sent to a girls home! Whaaaat??? I'm gonna miss her so much.

Lily is outta school now too, how am I going to survive without her?! First Krissy leaves, then my Lily and now Robin too??

Rebecca is back which is cool, not the same as Kris and Lily... But still cool. Well I g/g- ♥ Me

February 18th 1994 – Friday

Hi! Well a lot has happened and only in one day, or should I say night. Let's see, James and Dustin picked me up around 5pm. We went to James's, got Dave, then went to the packy, got a case of Bud and a pint of grain. Then went to Mitchell's house. Cory was there. And Nick came by later. The guys got totally trashed. Like Nick puked on Dave hahaha!! Like oh my God, what even?

Mitchell is a really nice guy. He doesn't seem like the others. He seems more mature, very quiet and looks like he's always in deep thought... James says that Mitch just holds everything in and is just full of pain, anger and hatred. I don't see that. To me he just looks lost or maybe lonely. But he seems to be a really nice guy.

Nick just kind of scares me. I mean not exactly scare but he gives me the creeps and I would never in all my life trust that guy.

Dustin is pretty cool, I mean he's Dustin... He's very laid back, funny and nice. Not to mention he is seriously one of the most talented musicians, EVER. Like for real. And his impressions! WOW!

Cory is a sweetheart. He's just really, sweet. I like him a lot.
He seems to have a kind soul. You can see it in his eyes. He's got
AMAZING hair! He's into all things nature. He's just, nice.

And of course Dave. He's so silly. He's a great guy, not very serious
about anything and only thinks for the moment. I don't know.
I could write more about him, but that's not really a conversation
for even here, oh gosh, nevermind, it isn't important.

I just thought it was about time I let you know who the people
we've been hanging around with so much.

Anyways, James and I were talking and I asked how many of
these people he thinks he'd stay friends with after school is done.
He said, definitely Dave. He also said something about never
quitting pot and I asked why was he telling me about the pot, I
hadn't asked.
And he goes, "I just wanna prepare you for the future."
I go, "Why? Do you see me there?"
"Honestly, I'll tell ya. I can see us together in five years getting
married. Actually I would marry you next year but I wanna go to
college and get everything set for you."
Then he kissed me and he goes, "I love you."
"I love you too."

"No. You don't understand. I love you a lot. I really love you..."

Then he goes, " I love you more every time I see you. (laugh laugh from me) No. Seriously. I do." Kiss, kiss.

He makes me so happy sometimes, it makes me forget the difficult ones. I really love him and I hope what he's saying is true.

But I just don't know where we are going and if it's together.

Oh yeah. I forgot when he was saying all this, I was getting embarrassed and thought, This isn't real, it's because of the drinking and as if he could read my mind or something, he goes,

"You might think this is the alcohol talking, but Emily, I'm telling the truth when I say it's coming from the soul."

I do love him. But aaaaaahhhh!! I just don't know!! ♥ Me

" ...oh no I've said too much, I haven't said enough. That's me in the corner. That's me in the spotlight losing my religion..." ~R.E.M

February 24 1994 – Thursday

I just found out that Krissy was in a car accident and was kill last night, early this morning. God, why did it have to be Kris!!
I can't handle this!! She was like one of my very best friends!! Why?? We were suppose to spend all summer together. We had talked about us eventually getting an apartment together and being roommates. I can't believe it. I just don't understand. Why Kris?? God, I love her like a sister. She was always there for me. Always caring and understanding.

Oh my God! I didn't even take her last phone call when she told Mom she was back in CT. I haven't talked to her since she was in Florida. I thought I would be seeing her soon. And now she's dead! And I will never be able to talk to her again!!

Oh my God. I can't believe it...

"She paints her eyes as black as night now.
Pulls those shades down tight.
Yeah, she gives a smile when the pain come
The pain gonna make everything alright..."

-Black Crows

February 25 1994 – Friday

This was the longest day in my whole life. I swear I was crying like every 10 mins if not more at school. I thought I was gonna die. I wanted to die.

Everyone was talking about it. People who didn't even know her were like all of a sudden her best friends!! And worse, people who had been mean to her oh so many times, said so much mean and hurtful things to her, about her, were also trying to act like they cared and had been her friends.

It's so messed up! FUCK THAT!!

And FUCK James!! James was just SO insensitive. Like oh well. It's no big deal! Shit happens. He actually laughed at how swollen my eyes were from crying all night!! Well fuck him!! How can he be so heartless? How can he not care? She was our friend and now she is dead!! What kind of monster is he? I feel like I am seeing him clearly for maybe the first time. And I HATE what I see!

I'm not in the mood to put up with this. Any of this.

I found out what happened. I'm trying to keep this short.

It hurts my heart thinking about it.

It was late. They had left the club. Krissy was in the back, and the car hit a patch of ice and then went head on into a semi-truck.

Kris flew out the back windshield, hit her head on the pavement, and bounced about five feet. Mark B, he was a senior last year, was there working night shift as an EMT for Newford Hospital. They were the first on site and he said that he held her hand and told her it would be alright, that so many people back home cared about her. She just looked at him and smiled. Then she closed her eyes and died.

I guess it's nice to know that she wasn't in much pain and her last thoughts were of us. The whole thing is still really hard to grasp. It doesn't seem real and at the same time all too real.
Anyway I spent the day over Amy's with Anne. The three of us cried. A lot. But we also laughed too. Remembering the good times. And there have been so many. I wish I had been better at keeping up in this thing. Now there's no record. Just a void on paper, and now in life for real where our Krissy once was.
I want to die.

Sunday is the wake, 6-8pm. I'm going. It's gonna be tough but I'll be able to handle it. I guess I have to. Well I really can't write anymore, so bye and I'll write more soon! ♥ – Me

P.S Bye Kris! We love you hun!

Kristen (Kris, Krissy) St. John

17 years old

May 7th 1976- February 24th 1994

"There I was drifting way out into the sunshine, expecting to crash but I'm tied to a string. Look at me, I'm a tangled puppet. I might be a mess but I'm sure can survive..."

-4 non blondes

2/27/1994

Kris

Her smile always filled us with happiness.

She could always make us forget the sadness.

She was always there when we needed a friend.

Always stood strong when the world took those unexpected bends.

She could always fill us with smiles.

Even when we were divided by miles.

She was always there when we needed a shoulder to cry upon.

She made us see when we thought we couldn't go on.

We will always remember the good and bad times we shared,

Remembering that she always cared.

Krissy, you will always be in our hearts,

And we will never, ever be truly apart.

March 11 1994 — Friday

GOD my life SUCKS! Its been more than a week since the wake
and the funeral. James didn't go with me. Didn't even offer.
Or even go on his own!! The whole thing was terrible.
The coffin was open and it didn't look like her. And it scared me.
I can't deal with her being dead. I can't sleep with the lights off
and I break down and cry A LOT!! I've been cutting again too.
But now I'm better at hiding it. I'll learn to deal with Kris's
death, I have to... It's just so hard! It's like my brain is trying to
reject the fact that she's gone. Forever.
I just... I just don't know.
James and I almost broke up. But I guess we're fine, for now.
I don't wanna go into detail about that, I am confused and angry
and hurt and just... I don't know.
I just can't deal with that or even think about it anymore.

But I do wanna go into detail about what happened tonight!
I still can't even believe it happened. Or that it's real.
I went out with Dave and James to Anne's house for a big party.
we were all just hanging out, here and there in different rooms
drinking. I had maybe two beers put together, we all know I'm a
lightweight.

James left the room to do whatever... And I asked Dave where his beer was because mine was all gone and for the first time in awhile I felt good, so I wanted more. I started looking around us, I leaned over and kind of on him. I had a very low cut shirt on, well lets just say he enjoyed the view. Then, and I don't know why, but I just looked at him and asked him to have an affair with me!! And he grabbed my ass!

Well James came back, so I just grabbed the beer next to Dave and sat back. James ended up spilling his guts, no his heart out to me and even cried... like I said, we haven't been doing great.

When we eventually had to go, Chad was bringing James and I home, I had to get my jacket outta Dave's car. We started talking and it leads to him grabbing my ass and working his way to my boobs! James came out for like a second and then had to get Chad from inside. That's when Dave went down my shirt and IN my bra!

I can't believe I let him! I'm soooo stupid! After James had told me he trusted me and Dave. That he trusts Dave with anything! Aaaahhh. I feel so bad! God. What am I gonna do?
I know, just keep it to myself and stay away from Dave.
The temptation is too great!

I know things haven't been great right now between me and James, and maybe even downright bad really.

But I do love James, we've been through a lot together in the last year. I don't know. Maybe he's too good for me.

What have I done? I hate myself for this. But the thing is,

if I am being truthful, I don't get the same tingly feeling I get when he touches me as I did when Dave did tonight.

I don't know...

"Women need a reason to have sex, men only need a place." ~Billy Crystal

March 13 1994 – Sunday

Well, its been two days and still I can't get Dave outta my mind!
I feel so bad, but it felt so good! Aaaaaahhhh! I don't know what
I'm gonna do. I told Kim everything and she was shocked!
Oh I wanna tell ya in more DETAIL what happened!
Honestly, I just want to write it all down just to keep it forever.
I keep thinking about it, over and over.

So James left Anne's room to piss and Dave was sitting kinda next
to me, up a little. He had had a beer, but it disappeared.
Like he was holding it and then not. I had a good buzz going and it
was dark in the room so I was a little confused. I was almost
crawling over him to find it and he kinda put his hands around my
waist.
Then for some reason I don't know why, I went right up close to
his ear and asked him if he wanted to have an affair with me. And
he looked at me, with the most gorgeous smile and goes, "Are you
serious?" I said I was. Then he grabbed my ass and goes
"Understand?" 'cuz Chad had just stumbled in the room and found
us. I said I did.
Well James came back and then he and Chad left the room again.
I had on a very low cut, tight body suit under a buttoned up

flannel. I asked Dave if he wanted to see it. Of course he said yes. I showed him, which seemed to make him very happy. I wish you could have seen his smile. God he's beautiful, especially when he grins like that. Well James came back and everything went back to normal.

Eventually we had to go and I had to get my jacket outta Dave's car because Chad was driving James and I home. So Dave and I went out to the cars. I got it, put it on and the next thing I know, Dave's arms were around my waist, hands on my ass. I put my arms around his neck. He goes, "I can't believe you're serious!" Then his hands go to my boobs. Both hands. He smiled and just caressed. We heard the door. So we stopped. It was James, and stupid me actually sent him back in the house to get Chad! Well, Dave comes up behind me (I'd like to mention he was hard!!) His arms were around my waist and I put my head back, kinda on his shoulder and he starts nibbling on my ear. Oh my god it felt so good. I was breathing pretty crazy, so was he. Well he starts moving around, then his hand goes to my stomach, traveling up fast and he goes in kinda a whispery breath, "Are my hands cold?'
"Yeah."
"Yeah? Do you want me to stop?"
He'd gotten to my chest and went in my shirt, into my bra and was caressing my boob!

And I go, "No"

"No?"

"No."

We were breathing pretty heavy by now, then we saw shadows by the window. And he goes, "If they come outside now we're pretty fucked. We better stop before they come out."

He backed up, moved over and goes, "Before clothes come off."

He was standing there and he goes, "I need a cool wind, a real cool wind." That made me giggle.

Then they came out and Chad, James and I left. Dave stood there and waved goodbye as we drove off with a big old smile and a mischievous sparkle in his eye that I know was because of me ☺

Oh yeah, I forgot. After James went in again to get Chad, I turned to Dave, undid 3 buttons on my flannel, enough to show off my shirt. I held out one of my straps just above where it connected to the actual bra lace part and go,

"My bra is black lace, see."

He goes, "Oh my God. Black lace."

"What's wrong? Don't you like black lace?"

"Oh God I like it."

Then that's when he came up behind me.

I'm such a damn bitch. Look what I did! I don't know what to do. I feel so guilty. But I also want more!!

The thing is, I've liked Dave since the beginning of 10th but Amy was going out with him. Then when they broke up I was already with James. Not to mention Amy HAD made Kris and I promise we would never "go for" him. Well boy did I go for him the other night.

What am I gonna do? I don't wanna lose James, its been shitty, but we were trying to work it out. And no matter what he makes me feel, I know Dave would only be a one night stand or so.
James wants forever. But do I?
I really don't know what to do, or what to think or feel.

I wish Kris was here. She would know what to do or at least stand by me in any decision I made, stupid or not.

March 18 1994

Well, its another Friday and another night over Anne's house with like 50 people. It was wild!!! Dave was there. Whoa!! God, he's so gorgeous!! We weren't doing too much at the party, just a bunch of coy flirting, but it was a fun time. Three people said I had a nice ass, so that made me feel good. I was happy, drunk but happy. Then a few other guys said a few other things too. But not important, after all they aren't Dave.

Anyways, on to the good stuff! Dustin brought James and Sara (his sister) home first, then he was gonna bring me home before he and Dave headed out again. Dave was sitting in front, but at the very first Stop Sign he jumped out and got into the back with me, saying he had to see if there were any 40s left. Dustin had to get gas, so we stopped at a station. While Dustin was inside paying and getting cigarettes, Dave went in my shirt again and we were just groping with clothes on.

Well next thing I know Dave turns my face to him and he kissed me... ummm WOW!!! It was so intense and amazing. He kisses like no one else. He held my face, tangled his fingers in my hair...

I can't even tell you how it made me feel. Well, we stopped cuz Dustin was coming back. We kept groping, slyly, as we went on the highway. He nibbled my ear and then he undid his pants.

Well we "groped" some more and not just over clothes!!!

We got to my house and Dustin let me out (he didn't see what was going on!!). Dave got out on the other side and I went and gave him a hug goodbye and he goes "Good job! Whoa!" with this huge gorgeous smile on his face, his eyes were practically sparkling!!

Then I kissed him right there, and he kissed me back good!! Wow!!

What am I gonna do!!! AAAAHHHHHH!!! God, I'm confused!

He makes me feel something I didn't even know existed.

But I don't know!! Just WOW!!! HAND JOB!!!!

3/19/1994

In a State of Confusion

Surrendering to the temptation of desire,

Bewitched by sinful deception

And enchanted by the scorching fire.

Stuck in this blackened abyss of illusion.

Yet, seduced by longing and mystified

By this deceitful delusion.

Tormented by this agonizing craving,

Devoured by this erotic entanglement.

But still the intensity keeps blazing.

Captivated by this sinister passion,

Divided by betrayal and dazed

By this obscure action.

Entangled in a kaleidoscope of emotions.

Enticed by a Judas touch.

Momentarily forgetting the loving devotion.

Lusting what is forbidden.

Ignoring what is true.

Keeping it all hidden.

What else is there to do.

"God, I feel like hell tonight.
Tears of rage I cannot fight.
I'd be the last to help you understand.
Are you strong enough to be my man, my man?
Nothing's true and nothing's right,
So let me be alone tonight.
Cause you can't change the way I am.
Are you strong enough to be my man?
Lie to me, I promise I'll believe.
Lie to me, but please don't leave, don't leave.
I have a face I cannot show.
I make the rules up as I go.
Just try and love me if you can.
Are you strong enough to be my man..."

-Sheryl Crow

March 24 1994 – Thursday

Today was James's and mine one year anniversary. Kinda fucked up, but oh well, I don't know. We aren't "going out" anymore actually, but we're seeing each other. No big difference from before except commitment isn't as strong. We are "allowed" to see other people, though he's made it clear that this is my choice not his and that he doesn't understand why I need "attention from other guys".
I can't tell him its not "other guyS".
It's just one. And that ONE is his best friend.

There's been a lot less tension between us, since we kinda broke up. I still care about him and visa versa but we just couldn't take the tension. Plus, I don't think the love I feel for him is love-love.
I don't think, maybe, I was ever IN love with him but did feel love for him. If that even makes sense to anyone but me.

Or maybe this whole thing with Krissy just made my view of everything change. Anyways, I got him a Pink Floyd tape and a card. He got me a dozen roses with a red and blue carnation plus a mylar balloon, which is shaped like a heart and says I Love You. God, he is so nice some times. I don't deserve him. Or at the very least he doesn't deserve what we are doing to him behind his back. I don't know what is going on with Dave.

It matters what moment as to what it seems like. Sometimes I think he's really really into me, like may even have real feelings for me. But then the other times...

I just feel like just another toy or some girl to use. I don't know.

I guess I can't get too wrapped up in it. I mean I DID ask him to have an affair which implies no strings. But I don't know.

I feel like it's more. James and I DID break up. And it's not like Dave is in anything serious right now. We are getting together on Saturday so who knows.

I'll write more then!

Oh yeah! Wednesday was the first day of Group at school, which is basically like a messed up teen girl group therapy session once a week. A table party of broken freaks looking for understanding. We will alternate through all 7 class periods so we don't miss too much of one.

It helps to have somewhere to let things out. To be heard. To be listened to. There's so much I try to lock inside. I'm glad I'm in it!!

C- ya later ♥ — Me

March 26 1994 – Saturday

So a lot has happened. First Andre Jones is dead. Stabbed!!
I wasn't friends with him, but it's still scaring me. Listen, he died
on March 24th, Thursday at 2am! Compare it with Kris.
She died on February 24, Thursday at 1:45am. FUCKED UP!
Right?? Now I'm dreading April 24!! I can't take anymore death
or sadness.

I went out today at like 4:30pm. James and Dave picked me up in
Dave's "new-old" orange VW bus!! It's beautiful and CRAZY!!
Kinda like Dave I guess!
We went to James's and Dustin came over. I didn't think much
would happen, being at James's and all. But he just got a black
light, so all the lights went off. I was sitting on the couch with
Dave, we had a pillow on our laps kinda covering us. I went in his
pants and he went up my shirt right there on the couch! James
and Dustin didn't realize at all!! Then James went upstairs to eat
and Dustin went to the bathroom or to smoke a cigarette or
something. Which meant Dave and I were left alone in the dark.
We kissed and he sucked my boob!!! WOW!!
I don't even know what to say!! Well, we groped a little more until
we heard people coming back downstairs, so we stopped.

A few minutes later, Dustin and James went out to have a cigarette and Dave and I were alone again! He went in my pants and, ya know... We were making out pretty damn bad!! WOW!!!!!
I could feel his heart pounding. And I bet he could feel mine too!
Well, we heard the garage door so we knew they were coming back so we stopped but we held hands underneath the pillow!
HE took MY hand!!

Then we (Dave and I) went out to the garage to "have a cigarette" and we made out and he went in my pants again!!
It was getting pretty hot and heavy. Both breathing like crazy. Wow!! Well, we heard James coming out and we stopped. But let me tell you, BOTH of us had the uncontrollable shakes really bad!!!
If he hadn't come out, I don't know what would have happened!!

This whole situation is driving me crazy!! Dave's coming over tomorrow!! YAY!! But who knows what's gonna happen!!
☺ ♥ Me

Write More Tomorrow!!

3/29/1994

Why?

why when I think of him does my heart start to beat fast?
When I know whatever this is it will never last.
why when he looks at me do my hands begin to shake?
why when I look into his eyes does my heart feel like it's drowning
in a bottomless lake?

I can't let myself feel like this, because I know it's wrong.
Knowing it'll end like an old tragic love song.
I keep trying to deny what's going on inside of me.
This can't be love, I won't let it be!

I've been screwed over too many times before.

So why can't I just turn around, walk away and out the door.

So many things remind me of that pain.

I know it's impossible for him to feel the same.

For he has one of those hearts that will never be tamed.

My brain keeps telling me not to feel this way,

But unfortunately my heart has something else to say.

I guess it's time to try to forget what happened,

And just ignore the fact that my heart will be saddened.

April 17 1994

Dave did come over that Wednesday we went in his van and fucked around. Very nice that the van has curtains!! Funny thing about them? Bethany the Bitch made them hahaha! Bet she didn't think this would be their purpose haha!

On Easter he took me to church. Afterwards we fucked around again, in the church parking lot! Lord have mercy on our sinner souls.

Then that Tuesday at the Fireman's Fair (also before the fair, just to get at James because he's been such a jerk lately, both me and Sara finally gave in and smoked for the first time, for BOTH of us, with Dave!! Woah!) while James showed Sara where the bathrooms were. Dave and I ended up in the alley behind the bank. All sorts of touching and kissing. It was so hot!!

But I'm tired of being hidden, this taboo thing. So I asked him in a note what he wanted to do. He said he wants to wait until next year until we go public. After all James and Bethany are still in the school with us and that could get uncomfortable.

Of course now Bethany thinks we're too good of friends to just be friends. She's right, but still. Fuck her. They're not going out anymore. Not for a while now, so whatever nasty bitch.

All my friends hate her and are determined to stick up for me if she starts anything. As of right now she just glares at me a lot. Dave actually told her to cut it out at lunch the other day, in front of everyone, including her friends. She did not look happy.

It was awesome.

Oh yeah!!!! Lily had her baby!!! James and I went and saw her yesterday at the hospital! She's soooo cute!!

Emma May Thompson April 11, 1994 5:45pm 7pds 6oz

May 1st 1994 – Sunday

So much has happened. It's so crazy! Yesterday I was going to the Daffodil Festival with James, Chad, Kyle and Dave. We got there and decided not to stay cuz it sucked. It wasn't exactly a nice day out either so not much was going on there anyways.
We ended up going to the Overflow (Chad was meeting us there later). I'd like to add here, I was stoned and drunk off my ass!!
Of course just my luck, Kyle and Dave decided to hike the hard way up. The rocks way. NOT-fun! I fell once and now I have a huge bruise on my knee and on my thigh. But we made it.

Evan and Paul were already there with some freak girl I did not like very much, she was wicked obnoxious. Chad showed up and Paul decided to hand out trips (I don't do that). Well everyone but me and Dave were doing it, not actually sure why he didn't now that I think about it, but anyways more freaks came up and James was totally wasted and when he's like that he gets really stupid. Almost intolerable. All fucking horny and touchy feely, not knowing what personal space is, AT ALL. Plus he's a spitting close talker. Throw in the drunk googlie eyes and yuck!!
So I told him to please leave me alone. After all, I'm not his girlfriend anymore. Chad, Kyle and Dave went to the edge to watch the fireworks and James was talking to Evan so I went over to

the guys and sat next to Kyle. Well he's a little grope boy! I didn't really mind, it was pretty harmless. I definitely didn't get the tingles from him like with Dave. I think I would have kissed him if so many people weren't around, just to see. But nah. He's just not what I want. I ended up trading spaces so I was next to Dave. He and I started messing around, right there on the mountain, in the dark, on that rock because he had this BIG hole in his pants.

VERY convenient!!

James ended up coming over and Kyle and Chad decided to climb the tree behind us and throw branches down. Because, why not, I guess? Well one hit me right in the head and James FLIPPED out! When Chad came down the tree, James swung at him and they started to fight! In the confusion, and totally my own stupid fault, I got punched by James (was a total accident and wasn't even that hard). Finally they stopped. No one got hurt and they made up. But I was pissed. James was acting really fucking stupid.

He ended up feeling bad about Chad.

And while we were all just sitting there, talking it out, about 10mins after the thing, that's when Chad mentioned how I got hit in the shuffle and not him, like James thought. James just put his head down and closed his eyes. Like shut down. It was really freaky. I tried to talk to him but he wouldn't respond at all.

So I left him alone. I went to talk to Dave and Luke (who I might add here, also had very wandering hands!! Yuck!!)

But then I went back to James because he hadn't moved and we may not be a "thing" anymore but I was still worried about him so I go, "Are you OK?"

He looked up at me and my goodness, he was crying.

He goes, "I can't believe I hit you." I hugged him telling him it was OK and I knew he didn't mean to, it was an accident. I was in the way. But he just kept crying and saying there was no excuse, I don't ever deserve to get hit by anyone, and of all people him.

We just hugged for about 10 mins. Then he started to calmed down, so I left him to regain himself. It seemed that everything with all that was good. So the partying continued.

Later I just didn't want him to touch me and grope at me. He was just so drunk and gross. I mean he was wasted and cross eyed, plus we aren't together anymore, so I have every right to say no! Well he flipped and started yelling at me, saying he does all this shit for me, like rides and stuff. That I am leading him on because I just want to whore it up with other guys when he's just sitting there, the nice guy, waiting for me.

I was like, "Fuck you asshole!!" I mean, how dare he!! We broke up! And even if we didn't, if I don't want him to grope me, that is my choice!!

Why does he think he has say over my body more than I do?? And so what if he gives me rides! Am I a hooker who gets paid in rides or something?? No! I have plenty of friends who give me rides. I don't see them trying to force or shame me into anything sexual.

He makes me so mad!! And he wonders why I don't want to be with him. It goes well beyond what's going on with Dave. It's because of him and how he acts.

Well we had to leave cuz we had to hike down the (normal) trail and it takes like 15 mins so Dave, James and I headed on down the mountain. Dave and I groped all the way down! Yes, that's right hiking and groping all the way down a dark mountain. It was fabulous, it was MY choice and made me feel better. Stupid James.

On the way home in the car, James was driving, I was in the front and Dave was sitting behind me. He went under my jacket from behind. James couldn't tell a thing, or at least was too drunk and fucked up to notice. When we got to my house and Dave got out of the back so he could hop in the front seat, and damn was his dick out of his pants and huge! Oh baby I wanted him!! Right there, right then!

Well, we pretended to "talk" for a few minutes so that I could get a "handle" on things. Then he got in the car and I went inside, both with huge smiles on our faces.

Stupid James just waved goodbye.

He showed up today to apologize. About everything that happened between us on the mountain. I'm so confused. I love him... no, I loved him. And I don't want to hurt him, yet I think I am actually falling for Dave. For real... I don't know. Aaahhhhhhhh!

Oh yeah, haha, while we were still on the mountain I went over to Dave at one point and go, "I got a joke for you."

He goes "Ok."

"There's 3 types of orgasms.

The positive- Oh yes, oh yes.

The negative- Oh no, oh no.

And The fake- "Oh Dave, oh Dave"

He just smiled that magic smile and goes,

" I don't know about you little girl. You'll find out."

YES!!! I sure hope so!!

Oh shit! I almost forgot! James and a bunch of our friends are going to see Pink Floyd in MA in a couple weeks. He got an extra ticket for me. But it is on a school night so of course my parents said no. Well actually they said, "Absolutely not!"

It is SOOOO lame! This is a once in a life time opportunity that I am lucky enough to be around for AND to have some one ask me to go... This should be an experience I would never forget... now it will be something I will never forgive my parents for making me miss. Like HOW can they do this? At least Dave isn't going, maybe we can find SOMETHING to do to amuse ourselves hehe

5/16/1994

Woah?!

Once again I've played the fool.

I followed my heart and got screwed.

I told myself that it would happen again,

But I wouldn't listen.

Orange buses, yellow buses, purple buses, green buses...

Slowly going crazy, slowly dying.

Baseball hats and boxer shorts.

Flannels here, flannels there, flannels everywhere.

Inside my soul is dying,

But I always keep on smiling.

Brown and black, pink and white.

See the fish swimming?

Wow! This is nuts.

I feel silly.

Smoke a bowl, hit a bong... burnt!

Keep trying to pretend that it isn't real,

That the pain isn't near.

Car crashes and death,

Way beyond stress.

Let's play pool,

Boom! Click clack.

Pantera sucks and so does Mortal Kombat.

Go fuck yourself man!

Goatees... Or just the park, Janis Joplin or Collective Soul...

Crazy images pop up in my brain,

there is no way that I'm at all sane.

Bean bags or tv chairs.

Crazy little things to remind me that he really doesn't care.

Oh well, I say, just forget it and go on pretending

It doesn't mean anything at all.

5/16/1994

Fuck off!!

Fuck him!

Fuck everyone!

Everyone just go to hell!

Fuck love,

Fuck you!

I wanna die!!

Die, die, die!!

Rrrrrrr!!!

Full of rage!

Full of anger!

I don't care anymore!

Confusion sets in...

Oh well, just fuck it!

5/17/1994

Not for Real

I'm living inside a dream.

Things just aren't what they seem.

In my fantasy world we are together,

You and me forever.

You whisper to me all the things I want to hear.

Taking away all my sorrow and all my fear.

We are happy just me and you,

Kissing under a sky of blue.

Then this world is shattered,

Realizing that to you,

I don't really matter.

Inside my heart is being ripped and torn.

But towards you I'll never show my heartache and scorn.

It doesn't really matter anyways,

I'll always be happy for our few precious days.

" ...I need you like the flowers need the rain... I need you like the Winter needs the Spring... "
~America

5/17/1994

What?!

Two headed monsters who go to school.

Barney the dinosaur dropping dead.

Swirls of color swirling all around,

Blocking up reality

Both sight and sound.

Lucy in the Sky with Diamonds,

Flying up to the moon.

Monkeys running rampant.

Clowns on your stairs.

Show me the way to Sesame Street,

I've got a date with Big Bird.

Fishes are swimming around and around.

Going up?

No, I'm coming down.

Let's go for a drive somewhere fun.

Wonder Rat is in Australia

Stealing all the cheese.

Boom Boom up to the moon!

Look at these people who live in the stars.

"I'm a loser baby so why don't you kill me..."

Dork, go off and die!!

Little teddy bears are dancing in the hall,

The Dead have risen,

Long live the king,

And off with her head.

Flash, flash!

There goes the lightning

And here comes the thunder.

Stop that rap bebop stuff.

Here goes the bass.

Stop, stop, stop

I'm being driven' crazy...

Putt putt, woah.

No more gas.

June 18th 1994 – Saturday

Well a lot of shit has happened! Don't ask what's going on with Dave. Cause he's fucking with my head. BIG TIME! I mean, we were "together" Monday after school. And now he's pretty much ignoring me. All last night, at the Overflow, he was with Aubrey. They showed up together, they hung out mainly with each other. And granted I didn't see them get "friendly", but they did also leave together.

She is my friend, who KNOWS how I feel about him and what's been going on. So fuck her! Yeah, she's a really good fucking friend! Bitch!

That pisses me off. I'm so confused!

I don't know. Oh well life sucks!

I hate my life. Like he ever really cared. I want to die. For real.

" ...I want to be the girl with the most cake.
I love him so much it just turns to hate.
I fake it so real, I am beyond fake.
And someday, you will ache like I ache... "
~Hole

July 22nd 1994 – Friday

Its been more than a month and BOY has a lot happened.
I got my Lollapalooza ticket for the 3rd of August. $34.50!!
I'm suppose to go with James, Dave and Jim. We'll see.

From July 1- July 21st I was at Gram's while the family went to GA and FL to visit relatives. I didn't really want to go and they couldn't care less if I was around so... I guess it worked out.

I went out a lot with James, Dave, Esther, Cory and a bunch of other people. NOTHING is going on with me and Dave anymore. We have decided we are only friends. All everything was before was hormones and stupidity.

For the BIG shocker, James and I aren't even really talking right now. He's got a new girlfriend and I'm happy for him, I mean seriously it's about fucking time, but he's being an ass. He called me last Monday and goes, "Do you want to take a ride with me?"
I said yes and mentioned I was going out with Cory and Dave later.

He said he'd come get me and guess who never showed up!!
REALLY fucking mature! I mean he has a fucking girlfriend.

These are OUR friends. I'm not even "dating" or doing anything
with anyone EVER in front of him. Why won't he just stop acting
like a jealous jerk! I don't care other than the fact that now I
have to sell my Lollapalooza ticket cuz I don't want to go with
him!

Anyways, I kissed Rob at the Overflow about two weeks ago and
we were gonna "keep in touch" but we kept missing each other.
That kind of sucked.
I've gotten really close to Cory recently. We've been hanging out
A LOT. He's taking things way more seriously than me. But he's
really nice, and sweet.

Last night we (Cory, me, Mitchell, and Dustin) went to Max Creek
and I don't know how, but I ended up with Rob for an hour in the
baseball field.
We were just kissing. And he kept asking me for hugs, over and
over. We talked about how we both liked each other during school
but both were apparently too shy to say anything.

Then I kept thinking about Cory, and feeling really bad.

So I went back to where they all were. And we all just hung out. I have no idea. I like both of them. Aaahhhhhhhh!

 me- Emilee

(New spelling. I hate my stupid plain ugly name. It's not what I was suppose to have, Its never felt right. Thanks Dad for not being able to pronounce any other English names and thanks a lot Mom for not being willing to let me have a Vietnamese name. Boo! But maybe this new spelling will help a little bit.)

August 4th 1994

Went to RI for Lollapalooza yesterday with Dave, James and Jim.
It was WILD!! They got a party ball of beer. We drank and
smoked the whole way. And when we got almost there, we saw
this huge group of hippies. And for some reason James yelled for
them to all pile in the bus. Even though the rest of us were like,
NO!!
They all got in and it got super crowded, and hot.

And after we finally got in and parked... I PUKED! Eeewwww.
But it was all good after. We went in and saw all sorts of freaks.
Some girl changed her tampon RIGHT in the crowd. So gross.
It was insane. George Clinton was awesome. The Beastie Boys
were unforgettable. James was drunk and clingy. Yuck! Afterwards
we came back to town and hung out behind Kenny Rogers Roasters
with a couple of James's work friends. It was fun! Overall it was
a great time and I am so happy I went!
Still can't believe my parents let me go! I'll never forget it ☺

"Colors bleed to red, as I kiss your face.
Want to tell you I love you everyday, as we grow.
See I know now, yes I know now it's all my own. "

" ...Can you feel my pain as you walk on by... "

-Candlebox

8/28/1994

Reality

Crazy deceptions.

Lingering thoughts.

Forbidden feelings.

Alone in the world.

Looking past what is right

And turning to what is wrong.

Ignoring reality,

Living in fantasy.

Happiness is just another mask of illusion.

Confused beyond belief.

Not knowing what is truly desired.

A feeling of desertion and of aloneness,

Forever haunts me.

I feel on the brink of destruction and insanity.

Starting to realize I will forever

Be by myself, unloved.

September 18 1994 — Sunday

I guess you can say a lot has happened. I'm actually so tired of
having to say that.

Anyways, Dave and I hardly talk. Rob has another girlfriend.
But that's all fine with me. James's girlfriend is a major slut.
(my new friend Rose has known her for years, lets just say she has
a gift that if she passes it on to you, is the gift that just keeps
on giving and doesn't have a cure. Eeewww!) But I'm not about to
tell him, cuz he'll just accuse me of being a jealous ex.

Cory and I are "together", kind of- unofficially. But right now he's
in New Mexico and I miss him! We aren't "going out" or anything.
But he's already talking about getting an apartment together
when I graduate!! Crazy huh??
I mean he's a REALLY sweet guy, but my goodness, I don't know.
It's just all very serious.

I have no idea what is going on with anything.

Well I guess that's it... Oh yeah. I think I'm going CRAZY!!!

" ...It's wonderful how the surface ripples
But you're perfect, and I cannot breathe
Forever longing to make you mine
But I can't escape your stare.
Hold me closer, keep me near... "
~Faith No More

October 24 1994 – Monday

Once again I'm going to say A LOT has happened. But this time it's true. I'm living with my Gram and Uncle Tom now. That was a whole ordeal and I really don't want to relive it to write about it.... But basically I am now an orphan because my family pretty much thinks I am a worthless piece of shit. And they probably aren't wrong.

Dave and I are friends again. Rob is single and we're "talking" again. Cory was away for a month, and was just way more serious about things then I was. There was talk of moving to New Mexico and I don't know. I'm just not ready for that kinda thing.

Anyways, so then I refound Michael as a friend, then more. That ended up pretty bad. Let's face it, that ended even our friendship because I wouldn't sleep with him. I probably just should of... teach me to stand up for myself.

I guess I miss him? I tell everyone I hate him, but I don't. I don't know. I have no idea what or how I feel anymore. About anything. Everything is starting to just blur into swirls of rainbow colors, lit up trails, pain and smoke clouds.

I don't know who I am, what I am doing, or even what is real anymore...

Cory came back and I felt really bad cuz of the whole Michael thing. But Cory and I are starting to be buds again.

He also made it clear it wasn't too late for us. He's so sweet.

I am so horrible. My life is so fucked. I am so fucked up.

I don't know how much I can take.

Oh, my tongue is pierced now. So that's pretty neat.

Hurt like crazy, but I think I liked the pain.

Dude who did it was super scary! But it is wicked!!

November 20, 1994

Well, I finally did it... IT. Tonight. And with Dave! I don't know what to think. Or how to feel. It was weird.

I was high, like REALLY high. Higher than I have ever been before. Wooo was I feelin' good!

It was in his bus, in the sandpit behind my Gram's house, on a beanbag. I don't really remember too much of "it", it all just kinda... happened. Afterwards, we went to Cumbies and got chocolate milk. He's so funny. Then he brought me home. I don't know.

I am feeling sooooo much right now. But I am happy!
Maybe this will be the beginning of something new for us!

I g/g get some salad or something and then go to bed, it's so late it's technically morning! What a night!

"Do you mean what you say when no one is around?" ~Madonna

December 5 1994 – Monday

I'm still at Gram's. It's sometimes rough for many reasons.
But it's better than what home was like. So there's that.
I'm "with" Dave again. Though not in the open. Once again I am
his dirty little secret. But it seems different this time...

Almost more serious, maybe? I don't know. He calls sometimes and
even wants to see me when he knows we can't do "anything".
He even talks differently to me, acts different. I can't explain it.
I'm still scared though I don't wanna get hurt again.

I don't know. I'm happy, like so happy when I'm with him.
But I hate not being able to be "with him" in public. I feel like
he's ashamed of me. Or I am just not good enough for him.
Well I know I'm not, and I guess he does too since he keeps me
hidden and at a distance. The scariest part is, I believe I really
love him, for real. Like for real real. I don't know. I think I'm in
for a world of hurt. But I can't help it. I just can't stay away.

"...Years go by, will I choke on my tears 'til,
finally there is nothing left.
One more casualty..."
~Tori Amos

December 15th 1994

(just trying to get this off my chest and out of my head, not going to actually GIVE this to him)

Dave,

When I think of you, I find myself smiling and yet frowning at the same time. I never know what to expect. I buy your lies and excuses with no more than a knowing glance. Happy just to have you these brief times you allow me to have.

I gave you something special, that really means a lot to me, along with a part of my heart and soul. Sometimes I think I should just push you out of my life. But no matter how hard I try, I can't. You confuse me so bad. Never knowing what we have.

Sometimes it seems like you really care, but then, I don't know, it's like you're not even sure if you wanna be friends. Am I just a thing you come to because you know no matter how badly you treat me I'll always be here for you, willing to drop anything or anyone to do whatever you want me to?! Because no matter how mad I am, or how sad I get, that doesn't ever change.

My friends don't think you are worth it. But it isn't all bad. When we're together it seems so right! The way you hold me, the way we kiss, the things you say that mean so much. THAT'S what confuses me so bad.

I'm so lost. I am drowning. And no one can hear me scream. And honestly would anyone even care? Whenever I really sit down and think, it just makes me cry. Because honestly and truly, I'll tell you, my heart is full of your smile, and breaking with your lies.

But I still love you, no matter what. It seems the more I love you, the more I hate you for the pain I feel... yet everyday I continue to fall in love with you. I wish you'd be straightforward with me and tell me exactly what to expect, cuz I think I'm gonna go crazy if it keeps going on like this...

"...I sat there. If you want me I'll be here..."
~ The Cranberries

Undated

Shipwreck shitting down
Cobra (Hooded) Commanders throat
While smoking a joint.
Parrot is pecking at Cobra's back.

"...You know I love you,
but I just can't take this,
You know I love you,
but I'm playing for keeps,
Although I need you,
I'm not gonna make this,
You know I want to,
but I'm in too deep..."
~Genesis

1/1/95-Sunday

You will never believe what Sara and I did last night!!!!
I almost don't it was so whacked out.

Gram went with Ruby to a big old person party or something and then she was sleeping over. Haha. Can you imagine those two partying it up with all these Olds just gettin' funky alllll night long. Ha! Old freak rave hahaha. I mean it IS the two of them and we all know how wild and crazy they can get hootin' and hollering out the car at all the men no matter what age! Crazy fucking Bitties. I love them!

Well anyways, she was out at some rager and didn't get home until like 1pm today. WAY after I had already gotten back and showered. And Uncle Tom is in VT doing whatever it is he does. He won't be home for a couple more hours probably.

So, the last thing Gram yelled out at me and Sara was, "You can go to your party or wherever it is you are going. Just be careful. Don't be stupid. And do NOT even think of going to New York! I mean it girls!"

We just smiled sweetly and waved as the new Golden Girls took off. As soon as the car was out of sight we grabbed our stuff and went to meet up with this guy, Jordan, Sara just started working with at the gas station.

He's older, lives in Westville and told us his buddies and him were going to go to see the ball drop. TIME SQUARE!! So we went to his house. Smoked a J and then picked up some wine coolers.
Then we went to his buddies and all piled into Sara's car and someone elses and got the train.

Holy shit!!! It was so much fucking fun!!! The whole train was just one big party. Every single car!! We drank champagne, regular and pink, with complete strangers. We smoked bowls, Js, and blunts with faces we had no idea where they came from.

There was this one dude that looked like he was straight out of a Twisted Sister video just yelling MANIAC MANIAC over and over up and down the aisles. We were all cheering and whooping.
Dude pulled down a poster of a lion and ripped the face out and put his in it and started to ROAR at people!! Hahahha even the cop walking by was laughing. It was wild!!

Oh yeah and this Japanese like parent people were there just being all proper and cute, smiling and laughing at everything, snapping away on their camera. They saw my tongue ring and no joke, they posed with me with my tongue out and had Sara snap a picture!!! They're going to go back and show their family this crazy pierced mouth girl they met on a crazy train. "Going off the rails on a crazy train"!! And boy was it off the rails!

We got to the station and we decided since Gram had said not to go and we did, the least we could do is stay away from all the TV cameras that were everywhere on the streets.
Well as soon as we got out of Grand Central there were a few News channels filming the craziness. And what did we do???
Hahaha we both went right up into a camera and screamed in partying joy!!! So much for staying away from the cameras heheehe. But she's been home for like 3 hours and hasn't said a thing so I think we are in the clear ☺

So anyways we all walked in the streets, they were packed. No one cared that it was raining and cold. We were all out there to get fucked up, see a big bright ball fall, bringing in all the newness with it and washing away the shitty. We drank, smoked, walked. Got a slice of real NYC pizza. YUM!!! We wooped and yelled, and drank some more. One of the guys, John kissed me!

He's not really my type but hey, it was New Years Eve and I felt really good. So why not.

At one point we were all hanging out drinking and a cop says to Sara, "Throw out that bottle now! What are you like 15?"
His arms were crossed and he didn't look amused but also not motivated to do anything but make her get rid of it. Well Sara was NOT having it. According to her, he was "out of line" haha so the crazy wench just walked up to him, pointed her finger IN his face on her damn tiptoes and yells, "I'm not 15 thank you very much! IM 16!!" Jordan had to pull her away. The cop just shook his head and I laughed and laughed! I did a real lot of that last night. It felt fucking good. I haven't felt good in some time.

So we finally got to Time Square and we were all just huddled in, literally, the biggest fucking crowd in the ENTIRE world. John lit up a HUGE bat of a joint and we all passed it around. I got it, took a giant puff. Went to take another...

I look at my circle of people and they are all wide eyed laughing and pointing in my direction.
I was like "What? WHAT?"
Sara just bursts into the biggest belly laugh and says "Dude, look behind you!"

The crowd was packed in like sardines so I had been pretty much leaning on someone the whole time. I turned around and holy fucking sheep balls, it was a fucking cop!! He threw me the side eye and then continued on with his scanning of the insanity around him. I guess there were bigger fish to fry than a 17 year old smoking a zeppelin. Lucky me!

Anyways it seemed like within minutes of the ball dropping the streets were already mostly cleared. Of course there were freaks and drunks just scattered about stumbling, and tons and tons of garbage everywhere. Streamers, hats, noise makers, beer bottles. CONDOMS! Like I said., Everything.

Once we got back to the train, I don't know why, but all of a sudden Sara and I were just SO annoyed by the boys. Even though they are like 5 years older than us they were wicked immature. And it had been a really long night. And uggg, just enough.

We ended up moving to a different train car, after all Sara had drove so we knew we could get back home once we got back to CT. We let them figure out how they could all fit in that one tiny car they had and get back hahaha.

What a fucking amazing time. We had SO much fun. I hope I never forget just how much.

1995

New Notebook

PRIVATE!!!

"Enter the Realm of Understanding"
-Gravediggaz

1/29/1995

I got the idea to start a new journal from my friend Rose. It's a way to express my feelings and thoughts without bothering my friends and without keeping it all inside going crazy. I use to keep a diary but its been some time since I wrote last. Well not really that long honestly. But this is a journal not a diary. There's a difference. I can carry this around.

I suppose this is really going to be confusing cuz my thoughts are so jumbled. I also know this could be a very dangerous thing if certain people read it. But to be quite blunt, Fuck It! It's either risking the chance of people getting upset or my sanity.

I got dropped off at almost 12:30 noon this morning, after spending last night with Dave at Motel 6. Let me tell ya, my body is hurtin'! ☺ Boy does he make me happy, yet in certain ways makes me very upset and just so very sad. I love him. And I want him. I want him to be with me, I want him to need me, to love me, not just to want me one night here and there or just every once in awhile.

I want a goddamned relationship, I want him to hold my hand in public. Kiss me in front of people. Bring me out with his friends. But I don't think I'll ever get that from him.

I get really confused. Like, REALLY confused. I mean sometimes it seems that he really cares, when we sleep together, and I don't just mean the sex part, but the lying there together in the bed. The way he holds me, kisses me. The way he lays my hand on his chest and then puts his hand over mine. The way he caresses me while we're laying there together...

God I love him so much, but it hurts so much too. Why is he ashamed of me? Why am I so unworthy? Am I really just that disgusting?

I just don't know what to think or feel. I'm scared to think of what would happen in my mind and soul if he ends up with someone else. Oh my God would I die. I don't think I will be able to ever handle that. But I'm not really worried about THAT right now cuz I honestly just don't think he wants any "real" relationship. What really worries me most at this moment, is the PROM!

Cause I doubt he'll want to go with me when he could have anyone he wanted.

Why would he want ME! UGLY, FAT, STUPID me! I just know I won't be able to go there and see him with another girl, holding her, kissing her, knowing he'd probably be sleeping with her that night, knowing he really DOESN'T care about me. That I wasn't good enough to bring or be with.

I just wanna go somewhere far, far away so I don't have to see him with someone else. I don't know. I really wish he could/would love me. But I don't blame him. I'm hideous. I'm ashamed to be seen with me too. AAAAAAAHHHHHHHHHHH!!! My life sucks!

I just wish I knew if there was any chance of us getting together for real, even if it's not now but just maybe for real some time or if I am just being stupid. I mean of course there's that little glimpse of hope that still lurks inside deeply hidden in my heart, I mean he keeps coming back around. But that could just be because I let him do whatever he wants with me and no commitment, but hey this is all a chance I chose/choose to take. It's my choice to possibly get fucked over really hard. Of course it wasn't my choice to fall in love with him but...
As a song I once heard said, "I'd rather be a fool with a broken heart than someone who's never had a part of you..."
I live by that, because I will always cherish my time with him and the feelings I feel.

Well I could write on forever and ever about all of this, but...
I am still tired out from last night and this morning.
Peace, Love and Empathy, Later- Emilee

1/29/1995

Struggling

All I do is smile all through the day.

Hiding my feelings,

Throwing my sanity away.

It seems to everyone that my spirit is high.

But behind my mask of happiness,

I'm struggling to get by.

Death is all I think of,

To get rid of this hidden pain.

Tears of sorrow run down my cheeks,

Like warm spring rain.

Finally unable to take the pain anymore,

I walk with Death through his darkened one way door.

"I smoke two joints in the morning
I smoke two joints at night
I smoke two joints in the afternoon,
it makes me feel alright
I smoke two joints in time of peace,
and two in time of war
I smoke two joints before
I smoke two joints
and then I smoke two more"

-Sublime

1/30/1995 Monday morning- 2nd per.

Its only been one night since I wrote, yet here I am again. I feel like I have to write in this. Kinda like this notebook is my only real and true friend. How pitiful huh? It's like I can talk and talk to this (or in this case write and write), spill my heart out and I won't get any comments on how I'm stupid or whatever... or being interrupted by my friends problems. It's like someone just to listen to me. Someone who doesn't need me. Does that make sense?
I also hope that it doesn't sound selfish, cuz I'd like to think that I am not. I have a feeling that this notebook is gonna fill up really fast.

Anyways my body is still hurting, its my muscles and joints really. And I still haven't caught up on my sleep. This seems to happen all the time. Oh well, I suppose that's a sign of good sex! ☺
The other thing that always happens is an awkward depression that I go through. Which sucks. It's like I'm happy cuz I was with him but

3rd per
Ok, sorry I stopped mid sentence, but I'm in school so, TA-DA! That means work!

I'm doing really bad. I'm at the point right now where I'm gonna freak out over so much, how much can one girl handle!

I wanna just sit in a corner, rip at my hair and cry and cry.

It's taking all my will power at the moment not to burst into tears. I don't know. I'm so lost. I'm losing it really bad. Oh fuck everyone. I don't even care anymore. At this moment, I just want to die. It's just one of those damn things I guess. One of those things that just needs to be dealt with alone until it passes.

I mean I doubt I'd ever really kill myself, but I would find Krissy again... God I miss her.

A little less than a month and it will be a year and my heart is still so broken from losing her. But anyways...

I lost my train of thought dammit. I'm so tired, and I feel like shit. Not to mention my hip joints hurt like a mother fucker.

I have a question, well actually a few that keep running through my mind...

#1 Why can't I be happy?

#2 Why can't Dave love me?

#3 Why do I have to love him so much...

Write more later- Peace Love Empathy- Emilee

6th Per

I've gone through 4th and 5th without writing, WOW! Must be a new record of me not whining and feeling sorry for myself. Yay! Anyways, in lunch I told Sara that I wasn't going to the senior prom cuz I wouldn't be able to see Dave there with someone else and she goes, "Why wouldn't he go with you?"

Well, well, well let me tell you, I thought of 7 things:

1) I'm ugly

2) I'm fat

3) He could do a lot better

4) I'm not good enough

5) We're not public

6) He deserves better

7) I bet he's gonna go with Bethany or maybe even Aubrey...

YAY!!! Lucky me! I hate my life. Sometimes, well actually a lot of the times, I wonder if people would actually care if I was gone. For some reason I honestly don't think it would really matter to anyone. And that is upsetting. I don't know. I've been thinking maybe this journal isn't good. Maybe it makes me ponder my problems. Yet, I feel like maybe if I don't write, I'll blow up from keeping everything inside.

I don't know. I'm so confused. Aaaaaaahhh!! oh well... Later.

Peace Love and Empathy- Emilee

10:15pm

Well Sunday when Dave dropped me off he said he'd call either Sunday night or tonight and of course he didn't. I'm such a goddamn fool.

Also, I made a mistake this afternoon in 8th period English class. I was talking to Lily about Dave and our weekend. I forgot that Matthew, Bethany's brother was sitting there near us, and he was clearly listening. I hope it doesn't get back to Bethany that would definitely be a very bad thing.

Anyways, Lily was telling me that she thinks that I should just ask Dave out! HELL NO! He would laugh in my damn face.
I would LOVE to have a relationship with him, but I'm not THAT dumb. I know a lot better than that. Hey, sucks to be me.
Boy do I hate my life. But who even cares anyways...

Love- Me (10:44pm)

1/30/95

Untitled 1

There is a place hidden deep within my soul,
Where time and thoughts are irrelevant.
Where there is nothing but feelings.
Here, lying deep within holds so much;
Fear, love, pain, anger, strength...
Even forgiveness and also guilt.
Sometimes they swirl around and around
Getting entangled with one another
Until I can't even see,
Where I can't think,
And sometimes can no longer feel.
Through this spot
I see my life as a swirling tornado
That I cannot control,
Or stop, or even slow down.

All I can do is stand there

And watch as parts of my life,

Of my spirit and soul,

Of parts of me,

Blow through the endless sky

Like little shreds of paper

That no one, not even myself

Can catch.

1/31/1995 Tuesday

Period 1-

Today Tiffany and I were talking and she said, that I guess a few days ago, she saw Bethany and Dave at the movies together. According to her they looked "pretty cozy". YAY! Lucky me, just what I wanted to hear. I can't believe this. Isn't it just great! Why am I even surprised. And why will he go out with her in public, but never once me. Ever. Am I really that horrid? Am I really that embarrassing? I hate myself.

It's 6th per now. I guessed I skipped a few periods. Oops. Well since then I talked to Sara and Megan, they both think that I should just ask him out. HELL NO! I can't do that, cuz I think he'd just laugh in my face. I know if I was him I would. Ok, but to be honest the idea keeps running through my head. Maybe I'm just a glutton for punishment. I do wish he would just one day decide I was worth it and just choose me. Just once.

10:24pm-

I called Dave, he was suppose to call back and he didn't. But I saw him when I went to Dunkin Donuts with Elle and Megan. Anyways, I'm suppose to call him at 10:45pm. I don't think I will this time. I mean if he really wanted to talk to me, then he would have called back. Right? He probably won't be home and even if he is, I bet he wouldn't notice I don't call anyways. Fuck it!
I'm not calling. Screw it! I fucking hate my life!
From 9-10pm I had two friends call with their problems. Not that I mind cuz I really don't. But when do I get my chance to talk? I mean REALLY talk? I don't. And I am really struggling. They all expect me to know what to do. What to say. How they feel. What everyone else feels. And I CAN'T! I JUST CAN'T!! I can't even deal with my own problems! I'm honestly and truly sorry if it sounds selfish and all that shit... But how can I help other people when I can't help myself. Who the fuck is going to help me??
OH FUCK IT ALL!

Anyways, its 10:44pm. I should be calling him. Oh well. I heard some famous person once say something like, "You have to express your feelings and desires if you want something, if you don't, there's no way to achieve it. If you feel something for someone tell them, because they can't read your mind."

Ok, Ok. So nobody famous ever said that exact thing... but it sounds good and I got the idea from someone famous who said something like it, just not exactly it... but kinda? I just can't remember... I don't know! I can't even think straight anymore. But I guess it's right, no matter who said it or where ever it came from.

I suppose Dave doesn't know what I want or how I feel unless I tell him. Cause no one knows exactly what I feel except for me (and of course this notebook).
But ya know what? I can't say anything to him cuz I'm scared to know for sure that he doesn't feel the same, or at least I honestly don't think so. The thing is, I always expect Dave to know, just to know what I'm feeling and thinking, just to know when I'm pissed or hurt and to know why! That's not realistic.
But I CAN'T and WON'T tell him how I feel! Cause I don't wanna hear him say he doesn't care. I don't wanna hear anymore lies and most of all, I don't wanna lose what little I have with him.
I would die without my little time with him. I'm so scared.
And I'm not exactly sure why. I actually do wish I had the guts to tell him, to talk to him for real. Who knows, maybe.
I don't know. Someday.

11:14pm/peace love empathy Emilee

$#*%!

" ...You keep this love.
Thing (love), child (love), toy.
You keep this love.
Fist (love), scar (love), break.
You keep this love... "

Pantera

Undated

Everything started March 11 1994

First GREEN April 5 1994

First MIND Experience [☺] October 1st 1994

First TIME November 20 1994

" ...Feel my heart it's aching over...
...I feel so unsheltered
In my mind...
...I'm lost within your soul.
But I've worn all those patches in my dreams, always broken at the seams. Won't you help me... "

rm♥l26

2/1/1995 - Wednesday [Hump Day ☺]

Well, lets see... It's 2ⁿᵈ per and I just had homeroom and saw
Dave. He said he'd bring me to the clinic to get my pills. That's cool
I guess. I called him an ass and said I hated him and he goes,
" You never have anything nice to say, you always say such mean
things."
So I go, "OK I love you Dave, you are so nice and sweet. And I'm
just so in love with you!"
No I didn't say it seriously, I wouldn't dare!! Anyways he goes,
"Great!" and rolled his eyes.
I go, "what's that suppose to mean?"
He goes, "Like I believe that? It's all lies."
I just laughed at him cuz what was I suppose to say?
"OK, Dave, I am telling you the truth. I really DO love you, more
than you could ever imagine!"

I don't think so. I will never be able to do that, unless I get
really, REALLY drunk. But I have never drank enough to tell Dave
that I love him. Who knows, maybe one of these days.

Well I guess I'll pay attention to class now. Love, me

5:04pm

I'm home. And of course I'm thinking about Dave. But what's
new. Lily is determined to get me and him together! HA! Not gonna
happen!! She's said she's gonna go up to him and go, "So why don't
you and Emilee have a real relationship yet?" and go from there.
If she does do it, I guess I'll find out what's really happening.
Doubtful it will happen though. Thank God. 5:08pm.

5:35pm- He said to call at 5:30pm, I did. He's not home.
5:36pm- HE CALLED!! ☺

10:11pm

Well that time he called we didn't talk long, only about until 6pm,
than his mother needed the phone and he said call back in an hour.
I did, but he was eating. Then he called back in about an hour.
Well he called with an attitude. I don't know why! He was snapping
at everything I said, or had a snotty comeback. So for once I
talked back, I was just like, "Why do you have such an attitude
today."
He goes, "I don't have an attitude." in a really snotty voice. And
then he just got worse! So I go, " What is this? Is it like you call
me and give me shit cuz you know I will take it?" and all he could
do was laugh and then raise his voice all snotty at me about how
he didn't have an attitude. I started to cry and he got quiet.

Eventually he said if I wasn't going to talk than he was going to go. So I go, "What's there to talk about?"

He goes, "Fine. Goodbye." and just HUNG UP!

I don't know!! I was/am so hysterical. We are definitely fighting. I don't know! I'm so confused. Sometimes I think he cares and maybe, just maybe we have a future together. Then BAM he pretty much hates me! I'm so confused and honestly sick of going through this shit with him. I'm gonna have to be strong and actually demand that he tell me what his intentions are. Where I actually stand in his life. And where we are going, if anywhere. I will do it one of these days and I think sooner than later. It's time I stood up for myself, right?!?

I just love him so much. I don't wanna lose what little I have, even if it kills me. Cause I can't imagine my life without him. I wonder if he actually realizes exactly what he is doing, how much this all hurts me or how much I really do love him.

Maybe one of these days I'll have the courage to admit it to him. I have such a beautiful dream that I tell him and he tells me that he loves me too. That he just couldn't say it before and that we live together happily ever after. Not like anything like that would happen. But of course there's always hopes and dreams right? And who knows with a little faith... Damn. Who the hell do I think I am kidding? He will never want me for real.

" If you want to leave, I won't beg you to stay.
And if you gotta go darling
maybe it's better that way.
I'm gonna be strong, I'm gonna do fine.
Don't worry about this heart of mine.
Just walk out that door.
See if I care,
go on and go now but don't turn around cause
you're gonna see my heart breaking..."
~ Ace of Base

2/2/1995 – Thursday- Poem Time – ooooo! Fun!!

I've always been there when you needed me.

And I always will be no matter what.

Maybe I'm stupid.

Maybe I'm a fool.

But I'd rather have a little bit, than none of you.

(oh fuck this!! Nevermind! per 2. love, me)

"...I look him in his eyes but all he tells me is lies to keep me near...
...I'll keep giving loving 'til the day he pushes me away...
...Don't mess around with my affection..." -TLC

"And you look so fine when you lie.
It just don't show,
but I know which way the wind blows"

-Sublime

2/5/1995 -Sunday Night- 7:29pm

On Friday Dave and I pretty much made up I guess. I thought
we weren't talking and then Friday after 4ᵗʰ per I was walking by
and he goes, "Hey Woman. Did you call last night?"
"Yeah"
"Oh cuz I just found out this morning. Why did you call?"
"I wanted to talk."
"You didn't want to the other night."
"That's what I wanted to talk to you about. (DUH!) And well, I
still need to go to the clinic."
"You wanna go today?"
"OK."
"I'll call you after school."

Well guess who didn't call and was over James's playing video
games? (Sara called me.) He did it to me again.

I am such a fool. Why am I always the fool. 7:32pm

"Here I am different in this normal world.
Why did you tease me?
Made me feel upset.
Fucking stereotypes feeding their heads.
I am ugly.
Please just go away..."
~Korn

2/6/1995 Monday

Per 2.

You know I was thinking really hard today. I am ugly. Not just NOT pretty or not even just homely or plain. I'm really and honestly UGLY! There is nothing good about me! And that is very depressing. It scares me just thinking about myself, my whole self. I figure I could probably get A LOT of plastic surgery and be happy. I mean, look at me. My face is so Demented! And I'm overweight. I'm not totally FAT but... well yes I am. I just think I'm good at hiding it with my baggy clothes. And Dave. Well, he's just being nice when he says all that he says when we are alone together. I'm so putrid. I wanna cry. Any time I look in the mirror it depresses me. Sometimes I really wanna just rip out my hair and kill myself. I mean who is ever gonna love this monstrosity. I mean clearly Dave doesn't even want to be seen with me. I'm good for just behind closed doors. I am just so gross. Oh this really sucks. Write more later.

Per 7

Dave isn't here today. I guess I'll call him when I get home. I still need to go get my pills. And I think maybe we should finally have "The Talk"...

2/7/1995

2nd per. Dave called last night at 4:30pm and I wasn't home.
But I got a hold of him. I was outside at the payphone at Dunkin
Donuts, and he told me to go inside, because it was super cold, and
to call him when I got home. well I did but he was going out so he
said he'd try to call later. He didn't. Oh well. Life sucks and then
you die. I'm thinking about asking him to come over today so we
can talk. This is gonna be the breaking point. I'm going to ask him
where exactly this "relationship" is going. I need him to be honest.
I need to know where in his life I stand. I can't handle just being
here for his convenience anymore, hidden in the shadows like some
common whore.

It's making me crazy. Actually it's depressing me way too much.
I keep thinking back to when I first met him. It's so crazy.
I remember the 2nd day of high school he was in my homeroom
talking with Amy before the bell rang, reminding her of her
homework and books she needed, and from that moment on I knew
that he was the guy I could fall in love with in a heartbeat.
That smile, his hair, those eyes.

The fact that he was so caringly reminding her of stuff, carrying her books... He was perfection to me.

Another time while he was still going out with Amy. We were walking in the hall and I go, "That would be odd."

He goes, "What?"

"Odd"

"What?"

"Odd. O-D-D"

He goes, " Wouldn't it be O-O-D?"

"Aaah..."

Then he got this silly smile and goes, " No! That would be ood!"

He looked so cute!

You know what is on my mind a lot too? Amy once told me that Dave once wanted to ask me out but that was when him and her were having all their issues. Of course not sure why he would tell her that whether or not they were having problems. But I really wonder what I did to make him change his mind and decide I wasn't worthy of an actual relationship or even public knowledge.

But anyways, another thing that really sits on my mind a lot is the fact that Dave would actually "Go Out" with Amy (who he now hates) and with Bethany (eww), not to mention all the other girls he blatantly hooks up with and takes out places. But not me. Ever. That must show right there that he really doesn't care. That I'm not good enough. That I am in fact just a "fucking friend" and not worth anything more... maybe not even real friendship.

I don't know. But I do know I want to be more than that, than what we are. I want to be with him and just him. Oh well, "can't always get what you want"... bells gonna ring.

3rd per
I really wanna ask him all that stuff, but I'm not sure if I can. I just don't know.

4th per
I'm in Group. Just sitting. Fading into the background. Becoming invisible. How long before I actually fade away into nothing. I'm trying to think. Oooh what a challenge these days.
Dave is here today. But I haven't seen him.
I'll try later, I guess. I'm a little scared to talk to him.

6th per

I saw Dave. He said he was gonna call and Kyle asked if I wanted to go to the movies tonight with them and a big group from school. Ooooooo! Fun!!! But our plans never follow through. I always get left behind. So who knows, tonight could be different. It would be cool, but I don't see it happening. I guess we'll see. Write later.

"...I am confused,
fighting myself.
Wanting to give in,
needing your help.
Skin cold with fear,
feel it when we touch.
Outside I know you,
but inside I'm fucked..."
~Korn

Hump Day- 2/8/1995

I just had home room with Dave, Oooooo- do I love him!! He was
like, "Weren't you suppose to go last night?" So he DID notice!!
YAY!
The reason I didn't go was cuz neither Dave or Kyle drove, and
I'm not exactly friends with the rest of that group, the "cool"
kids. Anyways, for some reason I'm in a very hyper, yet bitchy
mood. It's kinda silly. I don't know. Dave said he might come over.

Yesterday when I saw him I told him I needed to talk to him and
he called after school and goes, "So what did you need to talk
about?"
I told him not over the phone that I'd tell him in person.
So today in homeroom he's like, "So what did you need to tell me?"
and I was like. "If I couldn't tell you on the phone why would I be
able to in home room?" (DUH!)

Then we were walking to 2nd period and he's like "Tell me"
and I was like "No. Can you come over today? Maybe? Cause if you
do, then I'll tell you."
" Well just tell me what its about?"

"No. IF you come over than I'll tell you!"

"Just tell me what its dealing with."

Then when he realized I wasn't saying a thing he kinda pouted. It was so cute! Anyways he MIGHT come over, then I have to actually tell him what I'm thinking. Oooooooooh- this is gonna be hard. Well g/g write more later.

7th per

Well I saw him again ☺ eeeeeeeeee!!! He makes me happy!! He's so silly! He might actually come over tonight. Hopefully around 5 or 6pm. Cause if I don't have the guts to talk to him, then at least I can physically harass him! I'm so sexually frustrated I can't think straight, so even if I can't make myself say what I need to... maybe at least I'll be able to not be frustrated anymore. Of course he never actually comes over when he says he's gonna, something always comes up. It would still be nice though. And maybe this time will be different.

Later 2/8/95

He didn't come over.

BROKEN

Thursday 2/9/95 -

Per 2

I'm in a bad mood today. A pretty depressed one actually. I'm not sure why. Well, yes I do. It's what it always is, Dave. I'm pretty sure it's clear where I stand. It's confirmed, I'm only a "Fucking Friend" and there's nothing else to it.

So I guess it just doesn't matter.
I mean... oh screw it. I just don't care. Yes I do. Too much. That's my problem, that I care too much and he doesn't care at all. I mean if he cared wouldn't he just call for the hell of it, or come over without me begging him too. Bring me out, anywhere? And that just doesn't happen. All I am to him is a person always available to screw when he wants sex. It's time I stop kidding myself. This "relationship" or whatever it is, isn't ever gonna go anywhere because he doesn't want it to. He doesn't want me. And that's that.

Well sucks to be me. But it's my own fault.
It's always my fault, just for being who I am. ♥ — Emilee

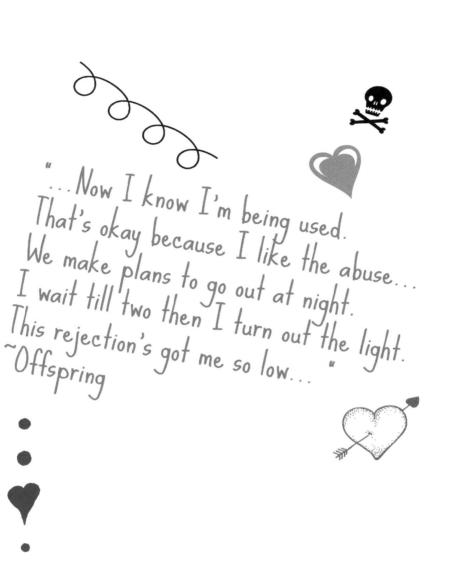

"...Now I know I'm being used.
That's okay because I like the abuse...
We make plans to go out at night.
I wait till two then I turn out the light.
This rejection's got me so low... "
~Offspring

Untitled 2

Hmmm? Thoughts run through my head,

I'm not sure what they are.

Feelings and emotions swimming through my mind,

And I'm fishing for a thought.

It's hard to comprehend,

Anything.

He is always on my mind.

I'm so confused and I don't understand.

It's always the same thing.

Does he really care?

Or is it just an act?

Is it like, well she's pouting and throwing a tantrum,

So I'll be nice to her for awhile,

Then everything will be fine.

Hmmm...

I found a new friend,

She's very dear to me.

She let me open her book of emotions and thoughts.

I understand her and I believe she gets me.

Crazy huh?

"When you say 'I love you' mean it."
~Life's Little Book of Instructions

2/10/1995 Friday

Dave came over and it was pretty much a waste of time if not a disaster! He came over and for like twenty minutes sat in my living room with my grandmother, watching the WALTONS.
Not even hardly talking and it was like 7pm.
I asked at like 7:05pm if he wanted to go have a cig, cuz he KNEW I needed to talk to him, and he just sat there like duh.
We didn't get outside and alone until 7:20 pm, then he tells me that he has to leave in 5 mins so if I'm gonna talk, talk.
I was like, "This is important! I need more than 5mins."
Then he got all pissy and was like blah I'm never coming over again! Blah blah, attitude attitude.
No one makes me so depressed or upset as him. He has no idea how hard this is for me. I need a little kindness and understanding from him. It's not easy to open your heart and soul to someone.

2nd per.
I saw him in between 1st and now, I was like, "What's up?"
He goes, "Nothing" in a blah attitude.
So I was like, "What's wrong? Are you mad at me?"
And he's like, "No!"

I was like, "Ok! I'll never ask you again."

He just got all snotty and was like, "I was just joking with you!"

But I was already upset! I HATE HIM SOOOOO MUCH JUST FOR FUCKING WITH MY HEAD!! It's not fair! And I can't take it anymore! I'm GOING CRAZY!! I can't take this shit.

Sara and I decided that he's just talented in fucking with people.

9/9

5th per

In 3rd per, which is Health class, we had a talk about "love". It was kinda weird. Anyways, Mr. Cameron said that he knew a "couple" where the guy was in control. Ya know like the girl called, the girl did everything, put in all the effort into the relationship. Well she got tired of the guy not responding to her, so she turned it around on him and eventually things worked out.

Maybe I should try that with Dave. The only thing that worries me is that he's not gonna respond. And that's going to be it, we'll be over and I can't take that. Oh I'm so confused! Maybe I won't try so hard with him for a while, see if he calls or makes a little effort, to see if he would actually care if I died or fell off the face of the earth. I don't know anymore.

♥ - Me

2/13/1995 – Monday

Well, I'm actually pretty happy. This weekend was pretty fun!
Friday was just there. Rose and I went out for awhile. She was
hunting for some bitch that crossed her. The chick is crazy!
Fun but wild!

Then Saturday I went out with her and Travis. And that's when
shit flew. Me and Travis got kinda cozy and that hurt Rose a
little bit. I feel bad because apparently she liked him (I had NO
idea!) but he told her that they were just friends and that's all
they would ever be and she said she was cool with that. But
clearly she wasn't. Nothing major happened, he held my hand in
Nobody Beats the Wiz and in the truck he had his hand on my knee
and I had my hand on his leg. Then he put his arm around me and
I laid my head on his shoulder. It wasn't a big deal. Anyways, I
still feel bad.
But she and I worked it out. So that's good.

Last night she brought me to meet this guy she thought I'd like.
I'm pretty sure she actually is just trying to keep me away from
Travis. Well this new guy was pretty cute and was really nice.

Rose told me that he said I was very pretty (I don't know what drugs he was on or maybe she was just lying). It made me feel special. But honestly, he's just not my type.

Then (this was a really good week so far) this morning Brandon said that this kid Vincent, that we met at a party said he thought I was pretty hot. So I'm kinda happy.

6th per.

Well, my happy mood is pretty gone! Too much thinking, too much in my head... I'm kind of depressed, because tomorrow is VALENTINE'S DAY and I'll be alone, by myself, once again.
I am so depressed. I hate being by myself, feeling unloved.
I probably won't even see any of my friends, NEVERMIND Dave.

7th per

So I saw Dave today and he was super nice. Not that he's ever really out right mean to me. He was just particularly nice today. But oh well, he didn't call ALL weekend. I called him but he didn't care to call back or whatever. Like he ever does...
I think that maybe I'll just give up the whole thing. I'm not calling any more, asking him over or going out of my way to see him in school. I just don't care anymore. I can't keep this up.
I'm gonna just be by myself for the rest of my life.
It may actually be less painful alone. ♥Emilee

(Still) 7th per.

I'm back and bored. Oooh! I am so depressed. I hate being by myself. It really pisses me off that people with someone special and people who love them, take it for granted. One day I suppose I will find someone who will love me. But I just want Dave. My heart hurts. AAAAHHHHHH!!

8th per.

I saw him. He didn't even say Hi. Great.

"...A wounded heart you gave.
My soul you took away.
Good intentions you had many,
I know you did.
I come from a place that hurts.
And God knows how I've cried.
And I never want to return,
never fall again..."
Janet Jackson

2/14/1995 – Valentines Day – Tuesday

2nd Per.

I called Dave yesterday. Yeah, yeah, yeah. I know I said I wasn't
going to anymore, but I am weak and I crave him. We talked for
about 30 mins. It was nice. Then I had to go. Anyways I wrote
him a note, telling him how I actually felt.
And I mean EVERYTHING! I wouldn't be surprised if he never
talked to me again. But I needed to do it. I can't keep it all inside
anymore. Or even just keep doing this like we have. It's actually
killing me, slowly and painfully. I just gave it to him before this
period. Sucks to be me. But at least he'll know. As they say,
" the ball is in his court" I know cuz I put it there and of my own
choosing, as scary as it was to do. And maybe that was stupid but
hey, that's the story of my life.

5th per.

Well, I saw him. Hmmm? Where to begin. Well after 3rd I almost
walked into him and he didn't say anything. He had this weird look
on his face, I can't explain it. I've never seen it before.
It was like he looked lost, confused? Something. He looked like a
little kid. I don't know how to explain it or what that means.
Then before this period I saw him while I was at my locker.

He actually stopped there to see me. Then, I don't know, we didn't really "talk" and especially not about the note.

Things just seemed uncomfortable and kind of awkward between us, but hey, at least he doesn't hate me. I'm not sure I could honestly deal with that. He means too much to me to lose.

Man, I can't believe I told him all of that. What was I thinking?! I'm such an idiot! Oh my God! I'm freaking out! Aaaaaahhhh!

I don't think I should have done that. I mean what the hell did I expect? Him to confess that he loved me too? (oh please!)

Did I expect him to not feel uncomfortable around me after reading all that gushy yuck??

I am such an ass! Oh my god! This sucks!

I'm gonna die. I want to die. I can't take this.

8th per-

I skipped last period because, I don't know, well because Dave has lunch then. He was really nice, but things are definitely different and tense kinda. He was picking on me.

Like I know he was joking and he always does that, but I just thought for once he could be serious with me. I poured my heart out to him and it doesn't seem to matter to him in the slightest.

I shouldn't be surprised. He's never serious with me, or about me.

2/17/1995 Friday   [☺] <----- NIGHT!!

Dave, you are my heart and my soul.

I live for you and I'd die for you.

You are the reason I cry.

And the reason I smile.

Oh never mind!

...And cover me, cause I've been branded.
I've lost my mind, lost my mind...

...Over me. You fade into the night.
Over me. You melt into the light.
Over me. You will fear the things I need...

...You never change, never change a fucking thing.
Not a, a fucking thing, but you - you'll cover me.
Give me shelter from the storm...

-Candlebox

2/22/1995 Wednesday VACATION!!!

It's going ok right now, for the most part, though my answer to that changes from moment to moment. I am so not right in the head. So much has happened.

On Friday I went to Lazer-palooza, it was great. As always.

Then Saturday, I went to a party with Sara and Megan. I met this guy there. He's 23. In the beginning I thought he was really cute and nice. And then I thought he was a good kisser. Boy was I stupid. It didn't end well. I don't want to talk about it. Ever. I'd rather pretend it never happened.

On Sunday, I found Dave, we slept together again. I know that sounds insane, but I just needed to do something to cancel out what happened. I needed to pretend everything is ok. And in his arms, it is.

I saw Dave Monday night too. I've been so happy to be near him. Spending time with him. It's almost like he could feel that I really needed him... If only he knew. If only anyone knew.

But they never will. It was my own fault. I kissed him. I went into that room with him. I just... I can't. No. Just move on. Like it never happened and just choose to be happy and enjoy being around Dave and my friends. I mean it's kinda just part of life sometimes isn't it? I know so many girls that have gone through all sorts of stuff like this. Or worse...

So suck it up buttercup, you aren't special and honestly, no one really cares about your pain, it's a downer.

Now I am waiting for Sara and Dave to pick me up, then we're going to get Megan. I'm happy. It's weird with what has happened, but there is no denying it, right now, as I write this, I am happy. Or at least for the most part. And that is all that matters. Now.

2/26/1995 Sunday- End of Vacation

Hmm? Where to start? Well we went to Portstown Wednesday after I wrote that and it was a total bomb. There was suppose to be some party that some guy Sara knew was having.
There was no party.

Our ride home was fun though. We played "Pa-Diddle" the WHOLE way home. Dave and I christened Sara's backseat ☺ WHILE she was driving! Later we dropped him off to go eat dinner. And the three of us girls went to another party which was definitely fun, but I wish Dave had gone too.

I didn't see or talk to Dave for the rest of the week.
Until tonight. We talked. Out and out serious.
I don't know, I don't wanna talk about it.

"I've always been in love with you.
I guess you've always know its true.
You took my love for granted, why oh why..."
Madonna

3/6/1995 Monday

I suppose a lot has happened. My uncle went to VT Friday and came home at about 11pm Sunday. My Gram left for Maine at like 9:30am Sunday. I woke up about 10:45am. I called Dave and asked if he was going to church. He said Maybe. I said I had to take a shower and he had to eat breakfast. So he said he'd call back. Around quarter of 12, he called and said he'd be over as soon as he could. He was over at 12:20pm.

Too late for church. Oh darn!

So we stayed at Gram's and it was great. We had sex in my house! In my grandmothers chair! And ya know what? While we were having sex, at that moment in time everything seemed soooooo perfect. I have NEVER felt what I felt at that moment, and I have felt a LOT. The feeling was sooooo strong I almost said "I Love You!" to him! Like it almost just burst out of me! THAT'S how intense it was.
I was talking to Elle, and she said if that was the first time I felt that, that strong, I was probably feeling some feelings from him. Boy do I hope so!

Anyways he had to go to work at 2pm. He didn't leave until 2:15pm! ☺ I made him late. Before he left he gave me a hug and said he'd call after work (about 7pm). He also said he had to leave then or he wouldn't ever leave! ☺

Well 7pm went by and 7:30pm... 8pm... and I thought, Damn he did it to me again. But at like 8:15pm there was a knock on the door... and TA-DA! There he was!! TWICE! He came over twice! He basically spent all day, except when he had to work, with me! For like the first hour we just hung out. Then we fucked around for awhile, then we spent another half hour or so just hanging. I loved it.

He stayed until quarter after 10pm! Then I walked him to the door. I was like, "Bye."
And he's like, "What you're just gonna stand there?"
I was like, "what?"
He goes, "Give me a hug you jerk!"

GOD I LOVE HIM!!!! Things are working out so much better than I ever thought. I'm so happy! I love him so much! ☺

3/7/1995- 11:33pm

Crazy perceptions of reality and fantasy.
Unable to grasp the concept of anything.
Afraid to feel, but unable to stop.
Is it that I'm not good enough for him.
My friends try to help,
but it's him I really need to hear
say those reassuring words...

"You said that I was naive, and I thought that I was strong
I thought, 'Hey, I can leave, I can leave.'
Now I know that I was wrong..." -Lisa Loeb

3/8/1995 Wednesday

2nd per.

My life sucks pretty bad. I'm in a mood. I guess the big problem is
I feel like my life is insignificant. I don't contribute anything good
to anyone. I sat there last night reading Elle's poems and
thoughts and realized that there isn't anything special about me.
I'm just here. She is so amazing and special. I am so not.
That makes me pretty sad.

And Dave, fuck. I don't know what happened between Sunday and
today. It seems like I'm never gonna understand him.
I don't know what I did wrong. I don't know if I even care
anymore. Nothing even matters.
I'm in such a pissy mood. Oh, fuck it.

4th per

I'm in lunch. I'm still pissy. Not many people notice though cuz I'm
so "cute and bubbly". Fuck that. I'm falling apart inside and no one
can see me dying right in front of them all.
Anyways, I still love Dave. C-ya

◇•◇•◇•◇•◇

3/14/1995 Tuesday

2nd per.

I suppose I'm neglecting you. Sorry.

Friday night I was [☺] and I wrote a note to Dave. I just wrote and wrote and wrote. I told him exactly how I felt. Everything. I mean I even wrote, "I love you" in it. I gave it to him yesterday night. Today he actually stopped by my locker to say Hi to me, asked me what was up and smiled. I thought he would hate me, or get scared and run for the hills. But I guess not. I think I'm pretty happy.

For the past two weeks I started to go to Mitchell's for band practice again. I love those guys. Cory isn't in the band anymore, but there's no hard feelings between him and the guys. Which is good. Cory still comes over and hangs out. I missed going there, I mean hey, I've been hanging out there since the beginning. They've gotten so good! And they have a gig the 31st! I can't wait. When they get famous I'm gonna sell a book about my experience with every band member. Hehehehe!

Ummm, oh yeah, this is so shitty. On the walk home last night from band practice, I ran into Chunk. He was telling me about how he is losing all sorts of "friends", getting called names and pushed around. All because he started wearing eyeliner and saying he is bi. It's really sad. He's so nice and people who were suppose to be his friends are just so cruel, this whole town can be. But he's planning on going in the Army soon so he'll be OK, I hope.

well g/g I ♥ Dave

SLIGHTLY BUZZED!!!

(the new band name)

Undated

Untitled 3

As I walk slowly home in the warm spring rain,

I walk away from where you are.

The rain stinging my cheeks.

My tears stinging my eyes.

Running down my face,

Consummating their pain.

The cars wiz by,

On this lonely street at night.

I try not to think about you,

But no matter how hard I try,

You keep invading my mind.

This may sound ridiculous to anyone but me,

But when we have sex

It's so much more.

To me, it is love.

Mother, did it need to be so high?-Pink Floyd

As I think of things that are happening or have happened.
I can't comprehend any of it. My life has taken some very
unexpected bends, taken a few sharp turns and almost hit one too
many trees. What's going on? A lot I suppose, or at least a lot to
me. But who am I? What am I? Nothing... Nothing but one stupid
teenager who is alone inside.

If people would think about it, our individual problems make no
difference to anyone not immediately around us. The women and
men across the world, they will never know my name or what I look
like or how I feel. Or think. If I die, it makes no difference to
them or anyone really. Life will continue, will go on. No matter if
I'm here or not. Everyone leaves everyone eventually, nothing is
forever.

I also think of me, of self perception. No one can ever argue that. It's an opinion, a personal belief. You should always respect others beliefs as long as they do no harm to others. They are to each their own.

And this is my opinion, my belief...

As I look in the mirror every morning, I feel sick. Sick for myself and sick for the people who have to look at this thing called a person.
It hurts me inside when my friends, being friends, tell me I'm not ugly. Of course they are going to say that, they're friends!
But I know the truth that they won't say.

Inside my mind, I think so many things about so much..

People think they know me. They think the way I dress and look makes me who I am. No! That's not right. I'm not who you think I am.

I am me, but ME is not Emily or Emilee. Me is someone different, someone who isn't sure where life will bring her.
What her purpose is... Her worth.

I am someone who is scared of so much. Someone who loves too much but is afraid to say anything in fear of the pain of rejection. I am someone who has so many thoughts but is scared to express them. I'm so scared of so much. I think I should find a room and lock myself in there forever, or at least my forever.

I don't ever want to be alone, it scares me to be by myself, to die by myself. All without love.

Love is all that matters. What makes life worthwhile.

I had love, or at least I had given someone my love. He took all I would give and threw it back in my face without a second thought. It hurt so bad and killed a certain spot in my heart. But he didn't kill the whole thing...though he all but crushed my trust in people. I met someone new. I don't know where it is going, or what it is, but he made me smile and seems to really just want to make me feel special.

I miss Dave at times, and some more than others...
But I will never want him back. I can't do that to myself anymore. It was, IS too painful. I am still not healed or whole from that, I don't know if I ever will be.

He knew me best out of a lot of people, most people. I miss him trying to help, trying to comfort me, just being around him, that smile...

But to BE with him again. No, I can't do that. I will never be able to forgive him for hurting me. For never outright choosing me.

I think deep inside, I will always love him... But now it's time to move forward and see where life takes me.

I can only hope that love will find me somewhere along the way.

1995

"And as we all play parts of tomorrow.
Some ways we'll work and other ways we'll play.

But I know we all can't stay here forever,
so I want to write my words on the face of today.

And then they'll paint it..."

-Blind Melon

1995

Dear Teenage Self,

Looking back is a tricky thing. Nostalgia can be a doubled edged sword. It can be so warm and comfortable, enveloping you in the coziness of what was and the familiar. The best moments that stay fresh in your mind, all those "firsts" that burn themselves into your soul for all time, making you smile those private smiles.

Then in the same breath it can shake you to the core and bring back things you thought were long healed to the surface. It can make you second guess moments, choices, decisions. Anything. Everything, if you aren't careful.

I am going to try my best writing this letter but it is definitely a bit overwhelming and proving way more so than I anticipated. I am not really sure where to start or what to say.

What an absolutely chaotic journey down the rabbit hole of the past. It was everything I expected and at the same time nothing like what I thought it would be.

Reading it through; I laughed, cried, cringed and smiled bigger than I have in ages. What a sad, needy, little girl just begging to be accepted, by anyone. To be loved, at all. To be chosen, to be first in someone's heart. What a lonely soul.

Some of it I remember, some I don't, and some I really wish I didn't. It is very surreal. Almost like it isn't ME on those pages but someone I once knew. Yet now, in hindsight and through those words written by HER, I don't think I knew her at all.

I guess that is kind of one of the underlying themes running throughout the whole thing. SHE didn't know herself either. Who was she when she wasn't trying to fit into a mold. Or even multiple molds. When she wasn't trying too hard to please everyone, and be a part of their lives? What did she do for herself?

Her likes and hobbies? Her talents explored, or maybe in this case, ignored. Who would she have become if she had looked beyond the need for outside validation and just loved herself for who she was and what she had to offer?

This is so crazy. Everything is SO serious and earth shattering at that point in life, or so it feels. I want to hug her. I want to tell her it will all be ok. I want to, honestly punch her at points, shake her a bit, and tell her to just shut up already. To re-freaking-lax. I don't want to hit her because I think she "deserves" it. But because I can physically feel that embarrassment of the blatant throwing of herself at people, in all types of relationships, in just amazing amounts of excess need.

No one likes a needy girl. They just don't, even though clearly in all cases, it just means that they do indeed NEED something. Yet it seems to have the opposite outcome.

I don't know. I should know better, violence is never the answer. Even imaginary. I also feel like I need to apologize to her for the amount of insensitivity she showed herself when dealing with so much mental and emotional struggles, on so many different levels and for many different reasons.

Just from these pages I can see pretty clear issues that are going on but just not really dealt with other than to deny or belittle herself for any of it: body dysmorphia, eating disorder, depression, self harm, anxiety, self medication, sexual assault, family turmoil, grief and who knows what else.

First and foremost, Sexual assault victims/survivors should NOT be taught to sucked it up. Or let go of it. People DO care. What is the "downer" is the fact that this is how we were raised to think.

That it was "normal" and that we should just deal with the pain, the mental anguish, the shame of violation... that it doesn't seem to have gotten much better in the years that have passed since.

Though, there are glimmers of hope with the amount of people who are voicing support and solidarity with and for all those affected. This is an issue that knows no boundaries and truly does need to be addressed.

It only takes one generation to change a mindset.

And just wow, I can not stress enough that suicide, and the thoughts of it should NOT EVER be something that is just dealt with until it passes. Geez. What the hell. No. Please. Go talk to someone. Anyone. Get help. Do NOT try to take it on your own. Can people get through it by themselves?

Sure. It IS possible. For some. But not for everyone and there is certainly NO reason to risk it or go through it alone. Talk to someone.

TALK TO SOMEONE♥

Mental health in general seems to be at least spoken about more commonly nowadays, albeit not enough and definitely lacking real life solution. But at least the dialog is open. If only we could really get it going and add the much needed: compassion, support, and connection that is so desperately needed by so many.

I know in my case there were many signs, many cries for help. The vast majority went unnoticed or never followed up.
Everything worked out in my case. Somehow.

It was definitely touch and go there for a time. Life got really really painful. I found myself wondering if the good out weighed the bad. And at moments, as it happens in life sometimes, there was serious question if it was worth it. But the answer always ended up being, and **ALWAYS** is...
Yes. Yes it IS worth it. All of it.

Our experiences bring us to where we are, make us who we are. Choices we make, curve balls thrown along the way, surprises, life events...
It's unpredictable. But isn't that what makes it exciting? Aren't the ups and downs, the twists and turns, the good and the bad, the painful and the joyful parts of this human existence what we are here to experience?

I wish I could say that it got better after that last entry back in Spring of 1995. I mean, eventually it did. But first it got worse for a bit. I know those journals are somewhere packed away, in boxes in the basement.
As well as compartments in my mind. I do not see them ever seeing the light of day, much less into something like this. After all, some things just aren't worth revisiting. Some things are just better left buried.

Thankfully, the "era that shall not be named", only lasted a very small amount of time in the grand scope of things. Although at the time it seemed like eternity. Now whenever it comes up, which is extremely rare, it's like remembering a dream or a movie I once saw. Lessons were learned but I cannot live dwelling on it, regretting it, or wishing it was different. It was what it was.

The only thing that can make you truly survive and not just exist is allowing yourself to heal, in whatever way works for you and then enjoying life for the beauty it has to offer. It is beyond difficult at first, but time does heal all wounds, if you allow it too.

Most importantly through experiencing that awful time in my life, the lowest of the low, I learned that I deserved respect and that when in an abusive relationship, the victim needs to know the following:

- It is **NEVER** your fault.
- You were not the one who **"made"** them do it.
- They **aren't** actually sorry.
- Drinking, drugs or depression is **NOT** an excuse.
- You **CAN** and **NEED** to get out.
- There are **multiple** avenues for help.
- **Reach out** to as many as possible.
- You **are** worth more than your abuser wants you to realize.
- You **are** loved, just **not** by them.
- Abuse is **not** love, in fact it **is** the absence of.

Throughout it all I kept in touch with very few of my friends, that is something that happens when you find yourself in an abusive relationship. The first step is to disconnect the victim from their loved ones. Isolate them, it's easier to control. And control is everything to an abuser. Although, I had already started doing a pretty good job of that myself by the time we became a thing, as evident in the last few months of the entries.

It went from all about my friends and our misadventures to just about Dave and how I felt about him. Cringe worthy for sure. So it wasn't difficult for this new guy to get me away from my core circle of people and their prying eyes.

Rose was the only steady person I saw during the "dark times". After a couple months of seeing what was going on, she somehow made sure that Dave and I were back in contact and friends again. Was she hoping I would tell him or that maybe he would just figure it out. I still wonder about it to this day.

But for all her interfering, which at the time I was very upset about, I will be eternally grateful for, always. I never would have had the nerve. Especially then.

At first Dave and I would talk on the phone occasionally, visited each other on the down low a few times, which we always ended up having "moments" of various degrees during. But even those were fleeting. We both had chosen very different lives and paths.

After school and summer, he went away to college at our state university and I was in the slums of hell. Until that fateful evening, he was home for the weekend and called to just say Hi. I invited him over and we've been together ever since.

Of course it wasn't all as smooth and easy as "and they lived happily ever after..."
Nothing real is easy. But oh has it been worth it.
We definitely had old wounds that we had to contend with, growing up to do, and some stupidness along the way. This is the way of humans. We make choices. Sometimes these choices lead to wonderful amazement and other times, to mistakes and contrast.
It's all part of the learning and living experience.
Dave and I have close to 30 years of friendship, and almost as many since having crossed beyond that line. We have both changed so much since those days.

He has become such an amazing man. He is one of the most compassionate people I have ever met. Smart, funny, still sexy as hell. Oh, that smile still gets me every time and that twinkle in his eyes still rocks me to my core. The way he accepts me. Loves me. There is nothing like it.

It was kind of funny going through all this and reading parts to him. His view of it all is SO different.
Which just brings me back to feeling that embarrassment of just how needy I felt back then, how much I needed a commitment RIGHT THEN, how much I threw myself at him... Why couldn't I have just slowed down. and relaxed a little bit?

Hindsight is 20/20 right? Shoulda, coulda, woulda...

But that isn't the right place to dwell. It all worked out. Everything always does, even when it doesn't seem like it is. Some times the contrast of life is exactly what you need to get to where you want, where you need to be.

Here we are with two wonderful young adult children who we have great relationships with. We have built a life together, with each other, for each other and are working for the future we want as one. He is my best friend.

He makes me laugh. Makes me smile. We have so much fun together doing anything, everything, nothing...

We have survived more storms than we care to count, and have always come out into sunnier waters; happier, wiser, closer and more grateful than before for what we have.

At the end of every day, he is the person I want to tell everything to. Share my highs and my lows. The one I want to annoy and to annoy me for the rest of our lives. And THAT is true love.

After all this time we joke often about how we are almost the same person. How we can read each others moods and thoughts like they are our own. We finish each others sentences and have even caught ourselves on occasion dressing almost matching without even trying. Yes, it is obnoxious to us too. More than a few people who we have seen over the years from back in the day have said how we are "that" couple, you know the one that makes people simultaneously smile and roll their eyes.

One of my old friends once called us "fairy tale relationship goals" when I ran into her a few years ago at a store (it was SO awkward). And, although we are FAR from a fairy tale and no where even in the same realm of a perfect couple...

We ARE perfect for each other in all our imperfections.

There is no one else I would rather go through this insane ride called Life, than this man who knew me before I honestly knew myself.

The strange thing is, I thought this would be a story about a sad little girl who didn't fit in and who was unloved. A story about sadness and hurt... But that was just the ending to THAT part of Her story. The reality of it is, it was actually just the beginning of a real life love story.

I can happily report the my relationship with my family has drastically changed as well. It took time and understanding, not to mention forgiveness on all of our parts. The fact is, we all were doing the best we could at the time with what we had to give, what we knew and what we were "armed" with. Being a kid is really hard, but so is being a parent.

And of course, to this very day, my Gram is still my Gram. One of my very best friends and biggest and most constant supporters. There was a very small time that we did not talk after I left her house and entered into the "Dark Era". But thankfully that was only a very small blip in our overall amazing relationship. I love her so much. I wouldn't be the woman I am today without her and I will always be so very grateful for the relationship we have.

Thanks to the wonders of the internet and more specifically social media, many of the friends I had lost contact with, have been reconnected.

It's wonderful to see pictures of Amy and her husband with their son living down south. Just being happy.

Esther, who became a nurse, lives out west and is living life to the fullest as well as constantly accelerating herself forward in her career. She's come a long way from that single teen mother that was told she would never be anything.

Dustin is still a regular band mate of Dave's and still as talented as ever.

Elle has had many adventures, is married and has multiple books she is working on. She continues to be a guiding force in my writing. And we talk often, usually encouraging and supporting one another in our creative endeavors.

Rose and I stayed friends throughout everything. We lived together. Worked together at a few different jobs. She was at the births of my children. We became family.

Unfortunately, she was diagnosed with an extremely aggressive form of Multiple Sclerosis in 2006. She has been in a rehabilitation center for years, unable to walk or talk. It is more heartbreaking than I can express.

Lily and I found each other again YEARS ago and have been inseparable ever since. She is my soul sister. My person. She put herself through college and now has her dream job as a Librarian.She is happy, healthy, and her grown children are thriving. Every day she strives to be the best person she can be, and she is already pretty amazing. She is one of the most bad-ass people I have the honor of having in my life. I would be incomplete without her.

More recently, I have reconnected with Chunk, who was born Charles but is now Charli. Charli is not at all the sad and struggling boy from our youth. Now she is a stunning, confident and inspirational trans-woman. Charli was ALWAYS a gentle and fun soul, but there was also this deep sadness behind that smile we all knew and a longing in those beautiful eye. Not any longer! Now she radiates with light and happiness. It is absolutely amazing what a drastic change being accepted and loved for your real self can make.

There are others who I see here and there when I return to town ever so often to visit family, or as comments & photos on any one of the multitudes of social media platforms. Others still that I did not reconnect with, some I wish I hadn't, and a few I've never heard from or about again.

I do wonder where life has taken some of them occasionally. Funny how that works out. People who were once so important, end up being people you find yourself no longer relating to.

I, myself, have changed quite a bit since these words were originally written. I would like to think I am much more mentally healthy. The self loathing and self doubt hit an all time high in my 20's, However, somewhere in my early mid 30's I started to really "find" myself and in turn began to love and respect who I am... A Work In Progress. What a difference not hating yourself makes. What a change believing you have worth makes. I would be lying if I said I never have flashes of insecurities creep up. I do. Probably more often than I care to admit. But it's not even close to being in the same scope that it use to be.

I no longer mentally or physically abuse myself, thankfully for a long time. Nor do I believe the negative things I once thought not only about myself but life and the world in general. I don't feel alone anymore. I don't feel unloved.

Even with the ups and downs that life and all its chaos bring, I am happy and grateful everyday for everything I have.

And that includes everything I've been through because each thing: the good, the bad, and all the in between has brought me "Here". And no matter where "Here" has been, is or will be.... if "Here,", is full of people who you love and love you back? Then I think, "Here", is pretty fucking wonderful🖤

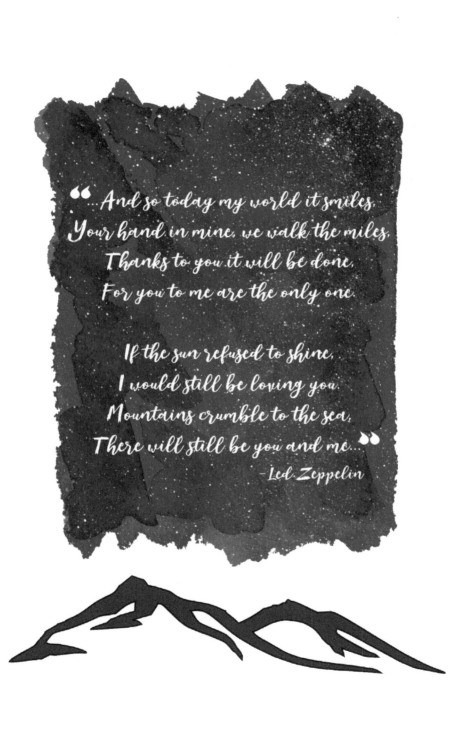

"...And so today my world it smiles,
Your hand in mine, we walk the miles,
Thanks to you it will be done,
For you to me are the only one.

If the sun refused to shine,
I would still be loving you.
Mountains crumble to the sea,
There will still be you and me..."

— Led Zeppelin

Cited Lyrics and Quotes:

*(date)- placement is the page before date

(date) - placement in that date

(date)* - placement after that date

(opening page) Kovac, Elle. "Alice". (2002)

*(May 6 1992) Nirvana. "Smells Like Teen Spirit", Nevermind. DGC, 1991. CASSETTE/CD/RADIO/MTV

(October 4 1992) Pink Floyd. "Mother", The Wall. Columbia (US), 1979 (US) CASSETTE/CD/RADIO/VHS

*(November 16th 1992) P.M. Dawn. "Set Adrift on Memory Bliss", Of the Heart, of the Soul, and of the Cross: The Utopian Experience.
Gee Street/Island, 1991. CASSETTE/CD/RADIO/MTV

*(February 2 1993) Leo Buscaglia. American Author. 1924-1998

(March 27 1993)* Bette Midler. "I've Still Got My Health", Beaches: Original Soundtrack Recording. Atlantic, 1988. CASSETTE/CD

*(May 21 1993) Oscar Wilde. "The Importance of Being Earnest". 1895.

(May 23 93)* Queensryche. "Silent Lucidity", Empire. EMI America, 1990. CASSETTE/CD/RADIO/MTV

*(June 20 1993) Grateful Dead. "Sugar Magnolia", American Beauty. Warner Bros, 1970 (US) CASSETTE/CD.

(July 7 93)* Beastie Boys. "So What'cha Want", Check Your Head. Capitol, 1992. CASSETTE/CD/RADIO/MTV

(Aug 25 93) Soul Asylum. "Runaway Train", Grave Dancers Union. Columbia, 1992. CASSETTE/CD/RADIO/MTV

*(Aug 28 93) Megadeth. "Sweating Bullets", Countdown to Extinction. Capitol, 1992 (US) CASSETTE/CD/RADIO/MTV

*(August 30 1993) Led Zeppelin. "Kashmir", Physical Graffiti. Swan Song, 1975 (US) CASSETTE/CD/RADIO

*(1/11/94) the Doors. "Waiting for the Sun", Morrison Hotel. Elektra, 1970.
VINYL RECORD/CASSETTE/CD

(Feb 18 94)* R.E.M. "Losing My Religion", Out of Time. Warner Bros,, 1991.
CASSETTE/CD/RADIO/MTV/VH1

*(Feb 25 1994) Black Crows. "She Talks to Angels", Shake Your Money Maker. Def American,
1990 (US) CASSETTE/CD/RADIO/MTV/VH1

*(2/27/94) 4 Non Blondes. "Drifting", Bigger, Better, Faster, More!. Interscope, 1992.
CASSETTE/CD

(March 11 1994)* Crystal, Billy. American Comedian as character Mitch Robbins. "City Slickers",
Castle Rock Entertainment/Nelson Entertainment/Face Productions/Sultan Entertainment, 1991.

*(March 24 1994) Sheryl Crow. "Strong Enough", Tuesday Night Music Club. A&M/Polydor, 1993.
CASSETTE/CD/RADIO/MTV/VH1

*(5/17/94) America. "I Need You", America. Warner Bros., 1972.
VINYL RECORD/CASSETTE/CD/RADIO

(5/17/94) Beck. "Loser", Mellow Gold. Bong Load Custom/DGC, 1993/1994.
CASSETTE/CD/RADIO/MTV

*(July 22nd 1994) Hole. "Doll Parts", Live Through This. DGC, 1994. CASSETTE/CD/RADIO/MTV

*(8/28/94) Candlebox. "Blossom", Candlebox. Maverick/Warner Bros., 1993. CASSETTE/CD

*(October 24 1994) Faith No More. "Underwater Love", The Real Thing. Slash/Reprise, 1989.
CASSETTE/CD

*(Dec 5 1994) Madonna. "Take a Bow", Bedtime Stories. Maverick/Sire/Warner Bros., 1994.
CASSETTE/CD/RADIO/MTV/VH1

*(Dec 15 1994) Tori Amos. "Silent All These Years", Little Earthquakes. Atlantic/EastWest, 1992
(US). CASSETTE/CD/RADIO/MTV/VH1

(Dec 15 1994)* The Cranberries. "Dreaming My Dreams", No Need To Argue. Island Records,
1994. CASSETTE/CD

*(1/1/95) Genesis. "In Too Deep", Invisible Touch. Atlantic/Virgin, 1987 (US).
CASSETTE/CD/RADIO/MTV/VH1

(1/1/95) Ozzy Osbourne. "Crazy Train", Blizzard of Ozz. Jet/Epic, 1980.
CASSETTE/CD/RADIO/MTV

(1/1995 - NEW NOTEBOOK COVER PAGE) Gravediggaz. "Diary of a Madman", 6 Feet Deep.
Gee Street, 1994. CASSETTE/CD

(1/29/1995) Maxine Nightingale. "Lead Me On", Lead Me On. Wingsong Records, 1978. VINYL RECORD/CASSETTE

*(1/30/1995) Sublime. "Smoke Two Joints", 40 oz to Freedom. Skunk, 1992 (US). CASSETTE/CD

(1/31/1995)* Pantera. "This Love", Vulgar Display of Power. Atco, 1992. CASSETTE/CD/RADIO/MTV

Undated 1995 *(2/1/1995) Candlebox. "Mother's Dream", Candlebox. Maverick/Warner Bros., 1993. CASSETTE/CD

*(2/2/1995) Ace of Base. "Don't Turn Around", The Sign. Eleni/Mega, 1993. CASSETTE/CD/RADIO/MTV/VH1

(2/2/1995) TLC. "No Scrubs", CrazySexyCool. LaFace/Arista, 1994. CASSETTE/CD/RADIO/MTV

*(2/5/1995) Sublime. "40 oz to Freedom", 40 oz to Freedom. Skunk, 1992 (US). CASSETTE/CD

*(2/6/1995) Korn. "Faget", Korn. Immortal/Epic, 1994. CASSETTE/CD

(2/7/1995) The Rolling Stones. "You Can't Always Get What You Want", Let It Bleed. Decca/London, 1969. VINYL RECORD/CASSETTE/CD/RADIO

(2/7/1995)* Korn. "Need To", Korn. Immortal/Epic, 1994. CASSETTE/CD

(2/9/1995)* The Offspring. "Self esteem", Smash. Epitaph, 1994. CASSETTE/CD/RADIO/MTV

*(2/10/1995) "Life's Little Instruction Book: 511 suggestions, observations, and reminders on how to live a happy and rewarding life", Brown Jr, H. Jackson. Rutledge Hill Press,1991.

*(2/14/1995) Janet Jackson. "Again", Janet. Virgin, 1993. CASSETTE/CD/RADIO/MTV/VH1

*(2/22/1995) Candlebox. "Cover Me", Candlebox. Maverick/Warner Bros., 1993. CASSETTE/CD

*(3/6/95) Madonna. "Take a Bow", Bedtime Stories. Maverick/Sire/Warner Bros., 1994. CASSETTE/CD/RADIO/MTV/VH1

*(3/8/95) Lisa Loeb and Nine Stories. "Stay (I Miss You)", Tails/ Reality Bites Soundtrack. RCA, 1994. CASSETTE/CD/RADIO/MTV/VH1

*(undated last entry 1995) Pink Floyd. "Mother", The Wall. Columbia (US), 1979 (US) CASSETTE/CD/RADIO/VHS

(undated last entry 1995)* Blind Melon. "Change", Blind Melon. Capitol, 1992. CASSETTE/CD/RADIO/MTV/VH1

(Very Last Page June 2019)* Led Zeppelin. "Thank You", Led Zeppelin ii, Atlantic. 1969 CASSETTE/CD/RADIO

Mentioned(not quoted):

(June 1, 1992) Nirvana-band

(April 22 1993) Shai. "If I Ever Fall In Love Again", ...If I Ever Fall in Love. Gasoline Alley/MCA, 1992. CASSETTE/CD/RADIO/MTV

(May 23 1993) Tyrant Trooper-band

(Aug 1993) Riders on the Storm-band

(September 19 1993) Aerosmith. "Angel", Permanent Vacation. Geffen, 1988. CASSETTE/CD/RADIO/MTV

(September 19 1993) Laser Zeppelin (as in Led Zeppelin music played to a laser show)-band

(5/16/1994) Pantera, Collective Soul-bands. Janis Joplin-musician

(5/17/1994) The Dead (as in the Grateful Dead)-band

(August 4th 1994) George Clinton-musician, Beastie Boys-band

Made in the USA
Columbia, SC
11 February 2023